Pro Rules

Pro Rules

*Creating a Solid Emotional Baseline
on and off the Tennis Court*

Andreea Ehritt-Vanc and
Stephan Ehritt-Vanc

with Rusty Fisher

iUniverse, Inc.
Bloomington

Pro Rules
Creating a Solid Emotional Baseline
On And Off the Tennis Court

iUniverse books may be ordered through booksellers or by contacting:

iUniverse
1663 Liberty Drive
Bloomington, IN 47403
www.iuniverse.com
1-800-Authors (1-800-288-4677)

ISBN: 978-1-4759-6375-5 (sc)
ISBN: 978-1-4759-6376-2 (e)

Library of Congress Control Number: 2012922090

Printed in the United States of America

iUniverse rev. date: 12/12/2012

Contents

— — — — — — — — — — —

Introduction

About the Book

What if you could control your emotions on and off the tennis court? What if you could approach tennis not as a *game* but as a *profession* that required as much discipline, if not more, as running a Fortune 500 company? What if you could act like a pro player even if you were in school or new to the game?

The fact is, tennis stars aren't always the most talented players on the court, but they are the most in control. They control their emotions, their reactions, their expectations, their confidence level, and their responses. They do get angry or hurt or emotional, but not to the point where they lose control. They react appropriately to a given situation and move on to play some more.

In tennis, of course, the baseline refers to the line at the end of the court, parallel with the net, that marks the "in" and "out" boundaries of play. In practice, we often line up on the baseline to run drills or sprints, but did you know that your emotions have a baseline as well?

In matches, the play always starts from the baseline. Every point of the match, the players start from there—it's the point from which you start.

If you have a good idea of what you want to do and a good idea of what to expect, you start from a solid base, or mental baseline.

When players have an optimal baseline (or a positive emotional default setting), they start a match in a balanced, calm, and focused way, full of alertness and far away from any emotional breaking point. In other words, they start on a solid emotional baseline. This helps them find, access, and get into the Zone—that perfect state of play—that *all* tennis players and coaches wish to achieve more and more often.

Players with a firm grasp of self, with a proper baseline, find that getting into the Zone becomes easier and more plentiful the more they control themselves, their game, and their emotions.

Pro Rules establishes a set of values that are optimal for your success. We don't think that the presented approach is the only or best way, but from our experience it is at least worthy of consideration. The approach is not for everyone, but if you choose to try it will prevent a lot of on- and off-court problems.

About the Authors

Brought to you by Stephan Ehritt-Vanc and Andreea Ehritt-Vanc, founders of the Pro-M International Tennis Academy, *Pro Rules* will help you have more control over your game, your future, and your career as a tennis player, because it will help you gain control over your emotions, your game, and your future.

Author Stephan Ehritt-Vanc worked for the Royal Dutch Tennis Federation (KNLTB) for sixteen years and is now working as the head of full-time programs of Pro M International on the ATP tour.

Coauthor Andreea Ehritt-Vanc turned pro in 1992 and finished her active career in 2008, stepping over to the coach's side of the net. Andreea has been the coach of Tamarine Tanasugarn from 2008 until today. Andreea is also responsible for physical programs and coaching in the Pro M International Academy.

While Stephan mainly evolved as a coach from the junior and educational part of the tennis spectrum, Andreea reached a Top World Ranking of 135 WTA in singles, and 40 WTA in doubles, winning several ITF tournament titles and two WTA titles. As a coach, her career highlights include two WTA titles and coaching the way to the quarterfinal in singles and semifinal in doubles at Wimbledon.

Over the last twelve years, these two authors have played and/or coached several players in more than sixty Grand Slams. Now they want to take the lessons of their combined years of experience to help other players achieve their goals and maximize their potential.

Not all who read *Pro Rules* will become Grand Slam players, but those who apply its principles will improve their play and, if they so desire, their professional rankings.

This approach might not make you better on your best day, but it will make you *more consistent, more often.* If you practice the *Pro Rules* in your daily life, you will find your growth becoming more stable and less limited by old boundaries.

That's because the goal of *Pro Rules* is to find your professional core, to learn control, and to master your game by following your own instincts with mastery and precision. *Pro Rules*'s ultimate message is a simple one: *Play the game, don't let the game play you.*

Who This Book Is For

Pro Rules is a book for players who choose to live a certain way. If you are somebody who wants to grow as a player, excel as a competitor, and mature as a person—inside and outside—then you will find what you're looking for in *Pro Rules*.

If you are in the inner circle of professional tennis, if you are an up-and-coming player (or an actual pro player), or if you're a parent, partner, coach, or friend of an up-and-coming player, then *Pro Rules* is for you too. This book is also for those who are passionate about tennis and want to understand more while watching a professional tennis match.

Your Emotional Baseline

Do you anger easily?

Do you often feel discouraged, helpless, fearful, or even out of control either on or off the court?

Do you lose points, games, and even entire matches because of your out-of-control emotions?

Does your opponent find it easy to psych you out once he or she discovers your fragile psyche?

These are the often-tough questions we face as professional tennis coaches every day, and the questions we urge even the most casual tennis players to ask themselves as well.

The best players are those who have learned to not only control their physical play, but their mental play as well. When you come up against a top player, chances are he or she is as tough mentally as he or she is physically.

In fact, *how you think* greatly affects *how you play*. Here's why:

We all start whatever it is we're doing from a certain place—it's our emotional default setting. Some of us know where this place is; we have worked actively to get there. Others were born more focused and calm in life, but whatever it is, this is our baseline in life, our starting position from which everything we do starts.

The more you know about where you are right now, today, the sooner you can tell how much work you're going to have to do to reach your goals.

For instance, if you're just starting out in tennis, you can tell your baseline right away compared to where you're playing in the matches, where you're "ranked." This is your professional baseline.

Where you are in your emotional development affects how you play, even the position you are ranked. If you lose your cool because your emotions are all over the place, well, you don't have a very solid baseline.

The default setting, or "baseline," of top players is one of complete dominance in the game, because they are in control—not the opponent, not the referee, not the weather, and not the surface of the court. Their control and dominance comes from an internal setting, an emotional "baseline," if you will, that helps them deal with any obstacle—even failure.

That's right, for better or worse, we all have an emotional baseline from where we start each day. Some people call it a default setting or their "natural disposition." You can see it in their general personalities—some are quick to anger, some are easygoing, some are studious and thoughtful, some are carefree and energetic. All start from their own personal baselines.

When you apply your emotions to tennis, you must adjust your baseline to find its most optimal condition. In other words, you must control your emotions, not the other way around. Of course, there are some things you can't control: your height, your reach, the length of your arms and legs. Other things you're not trying to control so much as enhance and even finesse. Every player has an individual, personal style. Our job as coaches isn't to break that style but to bring it out. Often it needs to be refined or tweaked to bring the full potential of the player out, but style is something we want to enhance, not downplay; it's one of the biggest aspects of a player's baseline.

When players have an optimal baseline, it helps them find, access, and get into the Zone—that perfect state of play—that *all* tennis players and coaches wish to achieve more and more often.

Players with a firm grasp of self—in other words, with a *proper mental "baseline"*—find that getting into the Zone becomes easier and more plentiful the more they control themselves, their game, and their emotions.

Establishing Your Baseline, on and off the Court

Pro Rules is focused on establishing a solid base from which to approach professional tennis in a *calm, natural,* and *focused* way. Both negative and positive emotions will always be at play in the world of tennis, but the strong player learns to take both in stride and, above all, react appropriately regardless of how he or she is "feeling."

It's not about "not feeling"; it's about dealing with the natural emotions that occur on and off the court in a more positive and effective way. Positive and negative emotions *will always be there* and *can always be there.* Your goal as a professional tennis player is to stay in the moment regardless.

The Zone is all about the moment, not the past or even the future but the present. Too many players are either anxious about the future or upset about the past, when neither really counts at the moment; all that counts is the present and how you respond right now, in real time, to what is going on in play.

Pro Rules uses your experience as a player and your respect for the game to help you enter the ultimate, meditative, and ideal state of play, or the Zone.

Living Life in the Zone

Remember, professional players strive to get into the Zone as often as possible; their life goal is to stay close to the Zone *at all times*. That's why having a firm grasp on where your baseline lies helps you get into the Zone, faster and more often.

The further you are away from your ideal mental and professional baseline, the harder it will be to find and enter the Zone. That's why much of this book is spent on building strong habits of body and mind so that you are always closer to the Zone.

Pro Rules helps you build habits to

- control your emotions;
- harness your experience;
- know your true value as a player;
- build your confidence;
- understand your baseline;
- understand your opponent;
- understand yourself.

All of these healthy, daily, and regular habits will help you establish a strong baseline so that you're never too far from the Zone in the first place. For those players who understand their baseline, staying close to the Zone in their daily life makes it easier to step into the Zone when they get on the court.

Pro players know that their emotions can be gateways to getting into the Zone, or barriers that prevent them from entering it. For instance, if they dwell on the past, are irritable or anxious, these unhealthy emotions prevent them from entering the Zone.

Just as significantly, being irritated and anxious in your daily life will prevent you from reaching being effective in the things you want to achieve, maybe even reaching your full potential. On the other hand, feeling confident about your skills and abilities can help you slip more quickly into the Zone.

What are the rules (baselines) of your daily life? If you emote easily *off the court*, you're going to take those baseline emotions with you *onto the court*.

That's why the life-play balance is so important in tennis; you can't really leave your "stuff" behind just because you've grabbed your racket and are standing on the real baseline.

Wherever you go, there you are.

To follow the way all the time and without slipping here and there is something that seems to be impossible, but getting closer and closer will minimize occurring problems and help players enter the Zone more quickly—and more often.

Pro Rules is based on five main elements that will help you play the game, and not let the game play you:

The First Element—*Experience:* Experience is the greatest teacher in the game. It helps you understand that there are the written rules of the game, the expectations you have about the game, what the press or your coaches think should/would happen in the game, and then there are what really matters: *the real rules of the game.* Things happen during a match that you can't really prepare for other than to accept, act on, and respond to them (see next element). These lessons come through experience and through living, learning, and loving the game. Consider the bad bounce; it happens. If you are a top player and you expect the ball to go one way and it goes the other thanks to a bad bounce, you have one of two options: use your experience to adapt to the situation, chase it down, and try your best to return it, or overreact, overdramatize, and simply give up. Players do it all the time. It's like they're thinking, "But it's supposed to go this way, not that way. I can't believe that ball didn't go exactly where it's supposed to go." Where it's "supposed" to go is one of the written rules of the game, but where a ball really bounces is the real rules of the game—and it's one that only experience can teach you!

The Second Element—*Acceptance-Action Response:* The Acceptance-Action Response is a two-part exercise in helping to stabilize your emotional baseline. First, *accept* the situation for what it is, not how it should be in an "ideal" world. Game play is much different than practice, and tournament play can be even more challenging than regular match play. What happens with your coach, on your home-court advantage, is not always how it will play out in a tournament or competitive match. In fact, it rarely is. Arguing about it or letting your emotions get the best of you will only make things worse; accept the current situation and "play the ball as it bounces." The second part of the Acceptance-Action Response is to *act*; act on the information you have, not some dream game you're playing in your head. You must accept *and* act to find the baseline that is right for you.

The Third Element—*Respect:* You must respect your opponent. You can't ever get too confident, let alone overconfident, by thinking you are superior to another player simply because you have a higher ranking (today anyway) than they do. For instance, just because a player has a lower rank than you doesn't mean he or she will play a less accomplished game than you. If anything, he or she might even be "hungrier" than you are and play a harder, more accomplished game! If you ever watch Roger Federer play against his opponents, no matter where they are ranked, he always approaches them as if this could be the time he is upset; he always gives them much respect on and off the court.

The Fourth Element—*Real Self-Confidence:* There is self-confidence and then there is *real self-confidence.* Generic self-confidence is often based on variables, intangibles that will change with the weather. For instance, rankings and competitors come and go. You may be "up" one day and "down" the next, so if you base your sense of self-confidence on a ranking or what they say about you in the newspaper or on some blog, you won't have "real" confidence, only temporary confidence. Know what you can do based on your current abilities, not your current rankings. This aspect of "real" self-confidence is so critical because it comes from within, not without. In other words, you determine how confident you feel based on your current known abilities, competitiveness, strengths, and weaknesses and not what some external message tells you to feel confident, or unconfident, about.

The Fifth Element—*Mastering the Zone:* The Zone is this perfect state of mind that a tennis player or pro sports player has when he or she is playing at his or her best. That doesn't happen that often, maybe one in every ten matches or so. But the good news is, the closer you stay to the Zone, the better your play is every time you step on the court. You don't arrive in the Zone by accident; you get there by mastery of play, and mastery of play is achieved by controlling your emotions and developing strong lifelong habits on and off the court.

Chapter 1: The First Element—Experience

Every one of us has different life experiences. Some of us learn from them; others simply keep repeating the same mistakes over and over. In tennis, as in life, how we use that experience is critical to our success.

As coaches, we can always tell when a player has potential, because although he or she may make mistakes, he or she learns from them. We may say something like, "Play a short angle cross court before you change direction down the line," and then perhaps spend the next few days practicing this short angle shot.

Some players, they can't—they won't—change no matter what. Not that this makes them "bad" players necessarily, but it makes them a challenge to coach. An open-minded player will at least give the lesson its due, will at least try it. If it works, great, next lesson. If it doesn't, they'll generally let us know why, or in some cases, they'll show us why. But the experience proves valuable because it adds to his or her complexity as a player.

Nothing Wrong with a Good Fight

Don't expect to win every time; do expect to improve every moment. Nobody wins every match, but the best players find something about every match to improve on before the next match.

Some days, we admit, a hard-won tennis match feels more like a bare-knuckle brawl. And, like any fight, sometimes you win, sometimes you lose. Strong players know that it's okay to lose, *if* you value the experience *and* put up a good fight.

There will always be a stronger player, bigger player, smaller player, or faster player, but that doesn't mean that player will always win. Sometimes those bigger players may be slower, or smaller players not as strong as you—it depends on how fiercely you're willing to fight for the win!

Take losing a match, for instance. No one likes to lose, ever. But even our top-ranked players recognize that there is something to gain from every lost match. It doesn't make them seek out a loss, exactly, and we all fight hard to win.

However, that's what good coaching is about. Good players evaluate every win, every loss, as if it's just their first, not their last. They might sit for hours afterward, later that night, even the next day and all next week, if necessary, correcting what went wrong, analyzing their play, training with their coaches to get a feel for what just went wrong, until they get it right.

Oftentimes we find that with many players, it's not any one specific thing that went wrong but a kind of habit of letting their emotions run their game, rather than the other way around.

So if they started losing, it really upset them to the point where they couldn't focus on their game anymore; all they could focus on was winning. While this is a good goal in theory, being preoccupied with winning puts the focus on the future, not the present.

In professional tennis, where we focus on the here and now, the future is too far away to control and the past has already happened. When we focus too far on the future or too far in the past, we lose sight of what's happening in the now.

The finite details of play—the game plan, the adjustments—get lost in the bigger picture of winning. Players stop keeping their eye on the ball or their mind on the plan, and start watching for the trophy instead.

One way to conquer this habit is to learn from the experience—to pinpoint the exact moment you stopped thinking about the match and analyzing where your emotions took you.

Emotions are difficult to control, but with experience we can learn to avoid some of the triggers or cues that make us angry, upset, resentful, or even vengeful.

Emotions are important in tennis because we don't play it alone. There is always an opponent in the mix, and a good one knows that for even the best players, unbalanced emotions are often their biggest weakness. A weak opponent can still win over a better player simply by being in control emotionally.

A common mistake of junior and lower-ranked future players is to judge players by their skills, not taking emotional stability into account. Doing this only gives you half a picture of your opponent. Professional players, on the other hand, look at the full picture of skills and weaknesses they are up against. Younger, less experienced players can easily get intimidated by the mere standing of a superior player, seeing him or her as perhaps "unbeatable." Pro players recognize that on any given day, in any given match, every player is beatable, particularly when emotions are involved.

Knowledge Is Power: The Seven Gifts of Experience

The goal of *Pro Rules* is to help you lead a more powerful, productive life—on and off the court. We're not in the business of self-help—we're not trained psychologists and we've never been on Dr. Phil—but we've coached enough top-ranked players to know that none of them leave their emotions behind when they step on the court.

What we do off the court affects our play on the court, and vice versa. The tennis court doesn't have an emotional force field around it that doesn't let in your anger, your anxiety, and even your fear.

And winning a match isn't simply as easy as leaving your emotions behind in your tennis bag on the sidelines. Our emotions are never too far from the surface. If you don't believe us, just try getting cut off in traffic. Your first instinct is generally to blow up, curse, and possibly seek revenge!

Emotions also strike close to home. We could spend the next dozen or so pages reeling off the long list of top-seeded players who have embarrassed themselves and their coaches by letting their emotions get the best of them on the tennis court. We can't stress enough how big a part emotions play in even the most talented players. You can have the strongest serve, the fastest legs, the most dominating return, eagle's eyes, and the stamina of an Olympian, but if you lose every other point because you're having a tantrum, blowup, or hissy fit, you'll still lose the match.

But don't just take our word for it. Here are seven other reasons why experience is so valuable when learning to control your emotions. We call them The Seven Gifts of Experience, and you'll soon find out why.

The First Gift of Experience: Perfection Doesn't Exist (but Excellence Does)

The most dangerous tennis player isn't one who seeks the "perfect" serve, the "ultimate" this, or the "platinum" that. Experience teaches us that even "best" is just a ranking. You can be "number one" this week and number ten the following week.

Rather than seeking perfection, we should seek excellence instead. Perfection is like a mirage we can never quite reach. Why? Because it doesn't exist. On the other hand, excellence is a state of mind that is continually evolving because it *does* exist. That's because excellence means that you are trying to excel above what just happened in your next action.

We achieve excellence when we are playing at our peak levels of performance: physically, emotionally, mentally, and technically. Have you ever watched a player walk onto the court, be in excellent physical condition, be calm and in control, and go on to dominate his or her opponent with precision, expertise, and skill? Even if he or she lost a point here or there, or even a game or set, you're seeing excellence in motion, because that player is in a peak performance state. It's something you can reach through training, mental and physical, but only when you give up on the unrealistic ideal of perfection.

The danger in seeking "perfection" is that we're doomed for failure if that's all we focus on. Let's say you're seeking the perfect match. Well, the minute you lose one point, that image of perfection is shattered. And then what? Now you will start getting the idea that it is less and less becoming a good day, and that things will go from bad to worse. This has you focusing more and more on the imperfection, and less and less on your game.

You can no longer have the "perfect" game, because your opponent has won that set. And yet if you're seeking excellence rather than perfection, you're still in the game, because you can get control of yourself and still go on to win the match.

The Second Gift of Experience: Every Opponent Is Different

The beauty of experience is that it teaches you the invisible element of any match: *who your opponent will be.* Many players make the mistake of training the same way because they have been successful like this in the past and now that they're doing well, they don't want to change a winning way.

The fact is, no training can be complete if it doesn't take the variable of a living, breathing, moving, and thinking opponent into account.

Of our training time, we spent 70 percent training "weapons" and 30 percent training to strengthen weaknesses. But because every day our opponents are looking for ways to avoid those weapons and reach our weaknesses, we have to be aware and adjust in the way we practice to be ready for these changes to be effective. Players have to improve, coaches have to improve, and the inner circle has to improve. That's the only way to keep evolving while climbing up in the ranking.

Even though you might have played the same player four times already, that player or you will try to change something today to alter the outcome of the match. Instead, before each match, ask yourself, "So, who do you think you are playing today?"

Truly great players know what they are doing to their opponent and know the way out. If the opponent doesn't find it, good. If he or she does, truly great players are prepared for the next adjustment to send their opponent back looking for solutions.

One of the greatest values—or "gifts"—of experience is the way it helps us adapt, improvise, be spontaneous, and overcome a truly challenging opponent. And not just those we've played before but those who have surprised us or challenged us or pushed us beyond our limits.

Competitive play is an opportunity to grow, expand, and adapt. The player who has stopped adapting or adjusting to his or her own performance—to his or her competitors, to his or her surroundings, to the crowd, even to the type of court he or she is playing on—has stopped growing. And, unfortunately, he or she is destined to stop winning as well.

Don't stop to smell the roses. Keep adjusting to stay ahead.

The Third Gift of Experience: Maturity

We can't stress enough the importance of maturity. But you might be surprised to find that maturity isn't at all related to age. Some of our youngest players handle defeat with as much grace as adults two or three times their age, while we've seen plenty of older veteran players who are simply too immature for their own good.

No, maturity doesn't have to do with your age; it has to do with your state of mind. It is also one of the primary "gifts" of experience. In other words, when you learn to stop reacting negatively to every bad bounce, bad call, or distracting noise on or off the court because you realize these are real parts of the game, you can play a stronger, more successful match of tennis.

You can tell an experienced player by the way he or she responds to stress or, more importantly, *how he or she avoids stress in the first place.* An inexperienced player will let stress get the better of him or her, whether this stress is self-created by his or her own lack of good play or, more commonly, by the way he or she perceives the situation he or she is in.

You can watch an immature player grow more and more frustrated over the course of the match, and you can bet his or her opponent can sense it as well. As this stress builds, his or her play suffers; it's like cause and effect in motion.

Meanwhile, a mature player—while far from perfect—is far more equipped to weather a rocky, even stressful match, by accepting, addressing, and ultimately controlling his or her emotions on and off the court.

Experience adds to maturity by teaching valuable lessons about

- handling stress;
- respecting one's opponent;
- knowing your own strengths and weaknesses, even your own limitations;
- understanding the "real" rules of the game;
- accepting the reality of the present tense versus the perfection of some future state;
- playing the game you're in, not the game you pictured being in.

The Fourth Gift of Experience: Strength

Strength is not just skin-deep. In fact, physical strength won't get you very far in tennis if you're not mentally strong as well. Experience gives you the "gift" of strength by helping you see the game for what it is: controlled chaos!

So many players think they can control the game, rather than spending time controlling themselves or, more importantly, their emotions. But how can you control

- a bad bounce;
- the weather;
- a broken string;
- a noisy crowd;
- a prejudicial line judge;
- a slow ball boy;
- the temperature?

The answer? You can't. And so rather than try to control those uncontrollable variables, the experienced player gains strength every time he or she stops trying to control the inevitable and simply plays through the variables that happen in every match.

That's why it's so important to recognize the vast and very important differences between the written rules of the game and the real rules of the game.

The written rules of the game exist in theory only. They dictate how tennis should be played in a perfect world, under ideal conditions, with opponents who play fair, balls that bounce in predictable patterns, and weather that always cooperates.

The real rules of the game? The real rules of tennis state the following:

- The sun will get in your eyes.
- The rain will make the court dangerous.
- The wind will influence the direction of the ball.

- Balls will bounce badly.
- Crowds will be noisy.
- Line judges will be less than perfect.
- Strings will break.
- The ball will hit the net.
- Competitors will (usually) be (a lot) stronger/smarter than you thought!

The difference is, players become stronger when they not only know the difference but also respect it and play through their emotions, the surprises, and the happenstance of real-world play.

The Fifth Gift of Experience: Knowledge

You might not naturally associate knowledge with the game of tennis, but it is a direct by-product of experience, and to watch a smart, wise, or knowledgeable player dominate a tennis match is to watch excellence unfold right in front of your eyes.

Knowledge comes directly from experience the same way strength comes from training. The more experience you gain, the more knowledge you accrue. Top tennis players become wise not just in the ways of the game but in the ways of fans, competitors, weather and bad bounces and all the unwritten "real" rules of a given match.

They have been here before, even if it's a new way of bouncing or a new competitor; they've dealt with adversity before, with tempers and strength and the games competitors will play to get you off your game.

That's the great thing about experience; it's transferable. You don't have to be playing on a clay court to know how to deal with a bad bounce, even if it bounces in a way—and in a direction—you've never encountered before.

The experience of having played a bad bounce before can give you the wisdom you needed to tackle the problem again, and again and again, without freaking out, losing it, or blowing your lid.

Wisdom isn't always readily apparent in great tennis players—that is, until you watch them in a stressful situation. Wise players can often dig themselves out of a devastating loss merely by keeping their cool, applying their experience, and readjusting their play to address the current conditions and/or their current opponent.

Wise players simply make wise choices. And choices are the groundwork for winning a match. Deciding to adjust on a bad bounce rather than standing there and watch it sail off left of court—it's a choice. Making the decision to keep your cool or blow off steam at a ref's bad call—that's another choice.

Losing a single point to a bad bounce may seem like just a point, but when it comes down to a tight match, that point could mean the difference between a win and a loss. Every choice brings you one point closer to success or failure.

And it all starts with wisdom, the kind of wisdom that comes only from experience.

The Sixth Gift of Experience: The Power of Identity

One of the most powerful lessons we can only learn through experience is that of identity who we are, how we are strong, and even how we are weak.

So many players know so little about themselves, it's scary. They believe both the hype about how good they are and the devastatingly powerful rumors that they aren't quite as good as they think they are.

So much of a player's identity is based on outside influences, such as

- his or her standing/ranking;
- his or her press, good or bad;
- his or her coach;
- his or her statistics (wins, losses, etc.);
- one good shot or match (which may or may not have been uploaded to YouTube for the whole world to see!);
- his or her reputation.

But the more experience you have on the court, in the game, the more you get to know yourself, the real you. So "they" say you've got a bad backhand. Playing your backhand more often can prove them right or wrong. Either way, the more you play, the stronger you get, and the smarter you adjust, the better you will be.

So "they" say you've got a killer serve. Do your stats back up the hype, or is it just that—hype? You'll never know until you get to know yourself better, and that's one of the many things experience can do for you.

Why is it so important to know yourself? Why is any of this so important? Can't you just turn off your mind and play the game? No, you can't turn your mind off, because your emotions follow you everywhere. They are always turned on; that's what fuels the little voice inside your head that can't ever seem to shut up, even in the most important match of your life!

The fact is, you can't escape yourself. Good or bad, you are the only thing you can count on once you step onto the court and approach that baseline. So the more you know yourself and the better you feel about yourself, the better you'll play and the happier you'll be with yourself.

The Seventh Gift of Experience: Control

Finally, experience teaches us one of the most important things we'll ever take with us onto the court: *control*. Matches often come down to control—not so much who can control the ball, or even the points, but who can control himself or herself.

Remember, there are so many things you can't control in a tennis match:

- the weather
- your opponent
- the ball
- the crowd
- the score
- the momentum
- the temperature
- the racket
- the court

But the one thing you can always control, the one thing you must always control, is yourself and the way you react and deal with these things. Experience can help. When every game is a learning experience, when every point is another piece of knowledge to be stored away, you gain a critical and important sense of self.

You learn how to predict your behavior and, as a result, control it. For instance, let's say you have a really bad temper when things start to go south. You know it, your coaches know it, and, thanks to YouTube, your opponents probably know it!

What can you do about it? Learn to control it—not right away, perhaps, and maybe not overnight, but you can begin to predict the behavior as you sense things getting out of control.

One bad shot might not set it off, but two? Three? Toss in a bad call and an opponent who's egging you on with little smirks and scowls? Now you're into the boiling point, but not if you can help it—and you can help it!

Experience will help you. You and your coach(es) can work on your temper in practice. You can do exercises to help control your breathing, learn techniques to rein in your anger, and even "count to ten" if necessary.

The fact is, control matters because it's often the deciding factor in a winning player and a losing player, in an amateur player and a pro. Have you ever seen a player lose his or her temper on the court? Once? Twice? Often? It doesn't necessarily make him or her a bad player.

We've all seen good, even great players completely "lose it" over a bad call or a shot they feel was in or out or some other real or perceived injustice. The fact is no matter how hard you try to control yourself, sometimes it just happens.

But imagine how much easier it would have been for those players to win their match if they hadn't blown up, lost their cool, and, as a result, lost their focus. Imagine how many points they lost as a direct result of that episode, because when you lose your control, it usually lasts a while—at least for a few points until you get your control back and start to play like your old self again.

A good opponent loves nothing more than for you to lose your control. Why? Because that makes his or her job easier; he or she only has to work half as hard to make a point because you're doing all the hard work for him or her. In fact, he or she will start working twice as hard to make this moment count and make it harder for you to regroup until he or she has you off the court.

The Pro Rules: Tips for Using Your Experience to Handle the Game's Most Common Problems

From bad bounces to bad calls, from courtside distractions such as mouthy crowd members to ball boys who don't know their place, here is a collection of the game's most common—and challenging—problems.

For each problem, we have provided a simple example you've probably had happen during one of your matches. Most come from one or more players we've worked with over the years, others from games we've played or simply observed. All are instantly recognizable.

After each problem, we provide an explanation of why this problem affects so many players but also why it's unhealthy to let it do so! Finally, we give you one of our "baseline rules" for how to act like a pro in this situation—or really, how to act like a pro in any situation.

Pro Rule #1: Bad Bounce

"Why is this happening to me?"

"But I'm winning. This can't happen *now!*"

"This is totally unexpected!"

"Just my luck!"

"Just when things were going so well!"

These are the typical, sometimes even hysterical, reactions of certain players when a ball bounces badly on the tennis court. By "certain" players, we mean inexperienced players. And who can blame them?

Young and even savvy players learn that if a ball lands here, it's usually going to go there, and nine out of ten times they'd be right. The problem comes that tenth time when they're wrong and the ball deviates just enough to disturb your first choice of action.

Decisions about what to do with the ball are made by pro players *before the ball bounces*, taking an expected trajectory into account. (They are not fixed; they are determined but still ready for adjustment.) This leaves only a fraction of a second to adjust if the bounce makes the first choice, an improbable option. In this split second they will choose the best remaining option to stay in play.

Why Bad Bounces Matter

One of the reasons why bad bounces "matter" so much is the emotional damage it can inflict on an inexperienced player. Far more than simply "missing the ball," if a player overreacts to this one lost point, it can mean a lost game, set, or entire match.

Emotions are like snowballs—they tend to roll downhill, not up. So if a player is surprised, perplexed, or even outraged by the happenstance of a bad bounce, he or she can overreact and really blow it. Blowing it only leads to more lost points, because, as we all know, it takes time to recover from an emotional outburst. Not only that, but a savvy opponent can undermine an otherwise-good player by realizing that anything outside the "norm" will set him or her off.

This sudden realization makes it open season on an inexperienced player's nerves and gives the opponent a decided advantage. In many ways, leaving your emotions exposed and letting them affect your physical game is literally like playing injured.

And all because one player took a bad bounce the wrong way.

On the other hand, an experienced player learns to recognize bad bounces—and, frankly, *all* the problems we'll discuss in this section—as part of the game.

Watch any professional match on TV and you'll see bad bounces happen at least a few times during the course of play. And very rarely do they mean the difference between a win and a loss. Why? Because experienced players know not only to expect them but how to handle them.

Strategies for Dealing with a Bad Bounce

Pro players—meaning those players who act like professionals even if they don't have a high rank or aren't in a Grand Slam tournament—react very, very differently than amateur players. They know that bad bounces will happen, and while they're never very pleasant, they still have to be dealt with.

Rather than freaking out, getting emotional, or "losing it," they do their best to respond within the limits of physics and then move on. If they lose a point, so be it, but they're not going to let their emotions escalate to the point where a single case of misfortune costs them an entire match.

In fact, pro players—experienced players—have certain "strategies" for dealing with a bad bounce. Here they are:

- **Accept it:** Bad bounces happen—that's all there is to it. They are one of the inevitable "real rules" of play. The best way—or, in many cases, when the laws of physics prevent you from physically returning the ball, the only way—to deal with a bad bounce is to accept it for what it is: an unhappy circumstance. Inexperienced players often try to control the uncontrollable, when what they should really concern themselves with is controlling themselves—namely, their own emotions.

- **Move forward:** The worst thing you can do after a bad bounce is dwell on it. Asking yourself, "Why did it happen?" or even "Why did it happen to me?" will only turn one lost point into two or three, or even an entirely lost match. If you're still thinking about a bad bounce six shots after it happened, then you're doing it wrong, giving your opponent every opportunity to do it right, and doing yourself in, in the process!

- **Reassess:** Oftentimes experience can turn a negative into a positive by taking the "bad" point lost in chasing down a bad bounce and turning it into a "win" by reassessing their game and approaching it differently. It's easy to get lulled into submission in a match that's going well or to let yourself "give up" in a match that isn't going so well. Sometimes a bad bounce—or some other on-court crisis—can "shock" us out of complacency and force us to "do better" or even fight back from being far behind.

- **Learn from it:** Finally, learn from the experience. That's what experience is, after all: learning from our mistakes, or even the "bad things" that happen to us. You can't predict where and when a ball will bounce badly, but you *can* predict that it's going to happen and be ready for it. That's what the most experienced players understand—and inexperienced players don't.

Pro Rule #2: the Bad Call

There is a big difference between how experienced and inexperienced players handle bad calls:

- screaming at the opponent
- screaming at the crowd
- screaming at the referee
- hitting balls over the fence
- penalty points
- disqualifications (and juniors who would have been disqualified on any tour event)

All these things—and more—happen a lot in lower ITF and junior tournaments. In other words, we see inexperienced players lose it at lot. They get irritated before the final decision, but, more importantly, they tend to lose it and keep losing it after the decision. They keep on with the discussions, pressing more, calling the head referee; you know how it goes.

Pros know. If the decision is made (the chair umpire checked the mark and called it out), there is really nothing you can do. No chair umpire will ever say after a discussion, "You know what, you are right; the ball *was* in."

So keeping the discussion and irritation alive after the final call simply isn't helping you or pleading your case very effectively. Accept the decision, for better or worse, and move on. Focus, adapt, and push forward. The next ball has to have quality to stay alive in the match. What's more, there is a fine line between venting your frustration and getting penalized for "losing it." We have seen these complaints go from warnings to penalty points and even defaults, which is why it's important for you to get back into control emotionally as fast as you can. We also see the inner circle of inexperienced players adding to the problem. If you are struggling for emotional control, it does not help if "your" people are screaming from the stands to keep the irritation alive.

On the pro tour, this does not happen as much. Pro players know that after the discussion, it's all about the next point, not whether you were right or wrong. And here is where inexperienced players get broken, lose sets, and sometimes lose even whole matches.

Why Bad Calls Matter

Bad calls matter for a variety of reasons. For one, an actual bad call can make you lose the game through no fault of your own. More importantly, when every point counts, being on the receiving end of a bad call can be emotionally upsetting. And, as we all know, bad emotions can lead to bad games.

Bad calls can also disrupt a player's momentum. The pace of a game is so critical to success or failure, and when that momentum is disrupted, even shattered, it's easy to lose one's grip—or just plain "lose," period.

Strategies for Dealing With a Bad Call

When faced with a bad call, there are a variety of simple strategies you can use to keep your eyes on the ball—and the prize:

- **Stay calm:** It can be hard to deal with a bad call, but blowing your temper is only going to make things worse. Yes, it may be unfair, or at least it may seem unfair, but what's done is done; all you can do now is control your emotions and play *from that point on.*

- **Stay focused:** One of the worst things you can do after a bad call is dwell on it, obsess about it, and fume about it. All these things fracture your focus and put you off your game—figuratively and literally. If the call sticks, all you can do is move forward—and to do so requires all your focus.

- **Follow procedure:** If you truly feel the call is in error, deal with it properly—by following the proper chain of command. For instance, you might ask the chair umpire to have a look at the mark. If he or she checks it and rules against you, that's it—there's nothing else you can do. Complaining more or approaching the head referee or opponent with more aggression or irritation will only escalate the situation and will not help in further dealings with the chair umpire or the opponent.

Pro Rule #3: Distracting Behavior of an Opponent

There will always be distractions on and off the court. These distractions are always present, but they don't always have to affect your play. In fact, the only difference between distractions is whether or not you give in to them.

The less experienced a player is, the more he or she tends to give in to distractions, even minor ones. In junior or lower-level tournament play, for instance, there is a very different vibe from the Association of Tennis Professionals (or "ATP") tournament play. At the lower levels, the atmosphere is very much "dog eat dog" and "only the strong survive."

Sometimes coaches encourage their players to be aggressive and have a "killer" mentality, and the rivalries between junior players at this level can be intense and unforgiving.

Tempers can flare under this type of pressure, words are often exchanged, and the rivalries, emotions, and flare-ups can happen anytime and anywhere—in the locker room, on the sidelines, and even on the court.

At the ATP level of play, the rivalries may still be intense, but if there are exchanges, they are usually an exchange of skills left on the tennis court.

Of course, no one—pro or amateur—is immune to emotions, but the difference between an inexperienced player and an experienced player is that the player with more experience has better learned to handle his or her emotions.

Why Distracting Opponent Behavior Matters

Let's say you have an antsy player who is jumping around courtside before the match, acting a little crazy or just spastic. Oftentimes in junior or lower-level play, an opponent will say, "Come on, calm down, keep still," or something to that effect. Words are often exchanged and tempers can flare before either player ever steps foot on the court.

Or you might have players who stamp their feet before every one of their opponent's serves, or do something else distracting.

Other strategies that junior and often inexperienced players will use to try to "psych out" their opponent include making the other player wait before every point, throwing them off on their serves or return.

In fact, junior players tend to use these "psych-out" strategies much more so than senior or pro-level players, who prefer to win over their opponents the old-fashioned way: through skill and skill alone. But mainly, pro players don't distract themselves with actively irritating opponents because it also takes focus away from their own level of play, and they know it can backfire when the effect of their irritation hurts them more than their opponent.

Strategies for Dealing with Distracting Behavior

To avoid losing your focus—or losing a match—due to the distracting behavior of an opponent, here are a few simple strategies to follow:

- **Ignore him or her:** It sounds too simple to be effective, but the fact you will rarely win if you allow your opponent to distract you. You have to be able to play despite distractions, and if your opponent is your biggest distraction, it's important to force yourself to ignore him or her.

- **Challenge yourself:** What can you control when everything else is out of control? The only answer is yourself. So when distracting behavior is making your opponent doubly effective, turn the focus inward and challenge yourself to play better despite his or her distractions. When an opponent finds out that his or her "psych-out" behavior isn't working, he or she will usually stop. It takes a lot of energy to both play tennis and wage mental warfare, and usually one makes the other suffer, so if it's not working, it's no longer worth it for him or her to persist with the distractions. Most pro players who irritate their opponents (intentionally or unintentionally) face opponents with a "fight to the death" mentality. At the junior level, irritating your opponent might result in loss of focus of your opponent. On the higher pro level, pros know that players will be difficult on the behavior level and are prepared for that, and for that reason they will even prepare better to survive any distraction that might be thrown at them.

Pro Rule #4: Bad Weather

There's no doubt that weather can adversely affect your play. Too cold, too hot, too wet—all these conditions don't just affect a player's comfort level, but the general conditions for play as well.

A wet ball can travel too slowly, or bounce weird, while a hot or even a cold court can speed things up—or slow them down—in ways few players can predict.

Generally, lower-level players are unprepared for playing in bad weather. Naturally, we all prefer to practice in ideal conditions, so to play in bad weather is strange for most of us.

When it comes to weather, the difference between an experienced player and an inexperienced player is often merely this: *preparation.*

Why Bad Weather Matters

When weather is bad enough, play ends, of course, but we're talking about weather that's just bad enough to hamper play but not end it. This can affect a player's shots in little ways.

You might not be able to play as aggressively when the court is damp or the ball is wet, you might not be at your best after four sets in sweltering heat. It's not enough to call the game, but it's enough to affect our game—often adversely.

Strategies for Dealing with Bad Weather

Weather happens and is completely out of our control. What is within our control is *how we respond to it*. These following simple strategies will help you deal with what's out of your control by taking control over yourself:

- **Predict:** Know what the weather's going to be like when you play. You may not be able to control the weather, but you can certainly predict it. Watch the news, watch the weather, and prepare accordingly.

- **Adjust:** If you know ahead of time (see above) what the weather is going to be like, you can adjust your game accordingly. So maybe a wet or damp court is going to slow the ball down. The top speed will be a bit down on your shots, so you might have to build up the points a bit differently. The worst thing you can do in bad weather is play the same way you do in good weather; you have to adjust your expectations and change your game to play as good, and hopefully better, and read the adjustments of your opponent and react to them effectively. Pro players know two things:

  1. **Bad weather conditions are the big equalizer.** If it is very hot, very wet, and especially very windy, the levels of players

get closer to each other. Time to adjust big time. The winner now, even more, will be not the one with the better ranking, but the one with the better adjustment. Start with adjusting your expectations.

2. **In extreme situations, you're game has to be different.** This can mean even from moment to moment. Forget about having a nice match or enjoying each point. It's all about getting the job done.

Pro Rule #5: Broken Strings

You'll often hear a junior-level player complaining, "Oh, man, I lost this one match because three of my strings broke!" Now, as coaches, we have all kinds of problems with a statement like this.

For one thing, no one should be losing matches over broken strings, particularly not three broken strings! If you played a match with three broken strings, that means you probably played with three used racquets and, in our opinion, there's simply no excuse for that.

In that case, it would be more accurate to say you lost the match because you simply didn't prepare well enough.

Why Broken Strings Matter

One broken string can alter play to the point where a point, or two, or even three are lost. That is, if you have to adjust a few more points to the new racket, that might be too different from the first racket.

What's particularly frustrating about playing a point with a broken string is that most of the time preparation—and experience—can prevent losing for this very simple, very avoidable reason.

Strategies for Dealing with a Broken String

If, and when, you are faced with one broken string—or three!—you will now at least have a few simple strategies to help you deal with this frustrating situation. Or, better yet, avoid it in the first place:

- **Prepare:** Pro players like Roger Federer and Rafael Nadal know that the only way to avoid a broken string is to prepare for the inevitable. If you watch such players closely, you'll see that every time they get new balls, every nine or eleven games, they'll also switch their racquets to make sure they're also using one with new string. In lower-level or junior tournament matches, this may not be necessary, but certainly a new racquet should be used at least every match to avoid the kind of lost points a bad or broken string can guarantee.

- **Be aware:** If a match is heating up and you're limping along on a tired racquet, yet you've still got some important points coming up, switch a racquet out before the string breaks. Experience increases our awareness because we've learned through trial and error to control the things we can, like broken strings.

In this case we used the example of broken racquet strings, but we might as well have been talking about any other material that breaks down once in a while (wet grips, wet wristbands, broken shoelaces, torn shoes, etc.). The message here is, be prepared to minimize the case of these things happening in big points, and be ready to adjust appropriately.

Pro Rule #6: Distractions around the Court (Audience, Ball Boys, etc.)

You can't allow others to control your game. This is the true mark of inexperience: letting others distract or upset you. On and off the court, you must keep your appearances up and act professionally and respectfully of other players, the referee, the audience, and especially yourself.

Pro players know that focusing when four hundred or more audience members are against you is not the easiest thing to do. Obviously, the more distractions there are, the less of a grip you have on control. However, the closer you are to your *baseline*, the more control you'll have over yourself, your play, and the outcome of the match.

Sometimes we see people in the crowd trying to influence the mind-set of one of the players. Sometimes these individuals are members of the inner circle of one of the players, trying to irritate the other player. Sometimes they are strangers who might not like you, or people who might have been betting against you on the Internet.

Why Distractions Matter

We sometimes even hear coaches encouraging their players to psych out the opponent, but this happens very little on the pro tour, and when it happens, the opponent mostly knows who will try it, making it less than effective, and oftentimes this effort turns against the players. On the pro tour very few coaches and trainers try this, and often it is also a sign of inexperience of the team around the player.

To the inexperienced player, distractions can be devastating. Their mental state is so vulnerable to a slow ball boy, a rowdy fan, or an opponent's "psych-out" strategy. And if a crowd, or an opponent, senses that a player is beginning to lose his or her cool, they will only increase the distractions to the point that many inexperienced and vulnerable young (or old) players simply shut down—or self-destruct.

Strategies for Dealing with Distractions

It is critical that players gain experience in the realm of dealing with distractions. Why? Because there will always be distractions, so the sooner you learn to deal with them, the better.

Here are several strategies for doing just that:

- **Focus on the present:** Don't worry about what happened during the last shot or how the crowd reacted. Focus on the here, the now, and what you can do to affect it positively.

- **Keep your momentum:** If you've got momentum before the distraction(s) start, work hard to keep it. If you don't have momentum when the distractions start, work to get some. Forward motion is the best thing you can use to distance yourself from the distractions you're facing. Focus on the next point, and be active in gaining the momentum for the next points.

- **Have a mental "win" in mind:** Sometimes seeing the *goal* can help you focus on achieving it. Distractions work best when you have no clear goal in mind, leaving your mind open to notice those things that a more focused individual might ignore.

- **Focus on the job at hand:** Keep your mind on the game plan and the adjustments that are needed *right now*. You might have to take your time before every point. Take your time until you have a clear idea of what you are going to do to win the next point.

Pro Rule #7: Be Prepared to Be Surprised

Relying on Expectations Can Make You Unprepared for Surprises, so Prepare to Adjust.

All top players have a game plan when stepping onto the court. For some, the game plan might be more detailed than others, but each top player knows his or her opponent and is prepared, through careful training, to beat him or her using an effective *game plan*.

The best players know that such plans are not—cannot— be written in stone. They may have to adjust their plan in accordance with their opponent's play.

For instance, maybe your opponent has been focusing on his or her backhand in the last few months since you've played him or her and/or watched him or her in a tournament. So you may have been prepared for a heavy forehand game. If you stick to that, you're going to get hammered, unless you adapt and adjust your game.

Junior or less experienced players, or even less experienced coaches, can go a year or more without checking up on the competition. But a lot can happen in a year. For instance, an opponent could have fixed a problem he or she had twelve months ago, or gotten faster, slower, stronger, or leaner. Anything could have happened, which is why experienced players know that the best way to avoid surprises is to *be prepared to be surprised*.

But being caught by surprise can really throw inexperienced players off. They can't adjust their plan because they have no backup plan. They keep working through the same mind-set: "Why isn't this working? Last year I beat him 6–1, 6–2, and now he's got me on the ropes. Why isn't this working?"

Other times inexperienced or lower-ranked players can have a plan, and the minute it starts to work, they abandon it because they get cocky. They think things like, "Well, this shot worked before, so even though it's not in the plan, I'll keep doing it because, hey, it worked once."

As we all know, getting cocky can seduce us to lose our perspective on what's really happening on the court, which may be quite different from how we're feeling after a few good shots. It's okay to hit some cool shots once in a while, but always keep focus on your "bread and butter" shots. If it gets tight, that's where you have to go.

Why Being Prepared Matters

Preparation is the key for success in so many matters—home, life, relationships, business, and particularly on the tennis court. Studying your opponents in real time, not just in the past (especially the far-distant past), helps you play them more effectively.

Knowing your own strengths and weaknesses helps you be prepared for what you can do to control your own fate, which is often the most critical way to be prepared.

Strategies for Dealing with Surprises

On and off the court, life is full of surprises. You can't prepare for every eventuality, but you can prepare to be prepared. In other words, the more aware you are that surprises will happen, the less surprised you'll be when they do happen!

The simple strategies below will help you prepare for surprises, even when you can't control them:

- **Be alert:** When you're alert, you're ready, and when you're ready, you can be ready for anything.

Yes, anything. As we've seen through this chapter, surprises are inevitable, but when you're alert, you can respond to them more favorably because you're not caught off guard.

- **Be adaptable:** You have to be ready to adapt, under any of the very real, very inevitable circumstances we've discussed here. Whether it's a bad bounce, bad weather, or a bad call, you can't just stick to the game plan because the game plan was for ideal conditions—and they don't exist anymore.

Parting Words about Experience

Experience is the greatest teacher in the game of tennis. It makes average players good and good players better. It turns losing games and puts them in the win column and moves ranks not by single digits but by double digits.

If you are careful, observant, and at all interested in becoming a better player, start becoming more observant right now—today. What you learn about yourself won't just surprise you, but if you apply it sincerely, it will make you a better tennis player.

Watch what happens, diligently, on and off the court. Watch tennis, live tennis, breathe tennis, talk tennis—play tennis. Observe your own play and the play of others with careful, patient, and sincere eyes. Don't just put in the time, but make the time to watch tennis carefully.

Don't just concern yourself with top-ranked players, or even winning players. We can often learn as much from how players lose—or, even better, why they lose—than we can watching a great player win. Great players make everything look easy; less powerful players are very transparent about what makes them less than great.

Sit on the sidelines and see how more experienced players react to the problems we've discussed here. See how they respond to, say, a bad bounce or even a bad call. What do they do when a string breaks or the sun is in their eyes or they're "forced" to play on a different type of court versus what they're used to?

Do they flare up and cuss up a storm? Throw their racket at the net and walk off the court in disgust? Not if they're any good, they don't. Chances are, they'll simply *accept* the situation, *act*, and *respond* accordingly.

And that's exactly what our next section is all about.

Chapter 2: Acceptance- Action Response

Have you ever rejected something you know to be true rather than simply facing the challenge head on and dealing with it? Relax, you're not alone. We do this all the time in life.

As children, we may get a bad report card and sit on it for days, even weeks, until our parents finally remember to ask us for it. Only then will we take it out and show it to them, suffering whatever consequences may await. Up to that point, we've been able to hide the bad grades, maybe even forget them, at least temporarily.

As adults, we may avoid getting the mail because we know a bill or collection letter is waiting. When we do get the mail, we may "bury" the bill, ignore it, or even tear it up and pretend we never saw it. We can put the pain of payment off for another month or so, but not much longer.

Eventually, whatever you deny is always going to find its way to the surface and affect your life. The adult way, the mature way, to deal with challenges and obstacles is to *accept* them and *act* on them with a positive response.

Tennis is no different. Rejecting the obvious and running from our troubles is no way to achieve your professional goals. What's more, owning up to your own personal weaknesses or facing opponents realistically is a faster, cleaner way to a more mature and reasonable baseline.

In this chapter we are going to talk about a two-step process we call the Acceptance-Action Response. The two steps are as follows:

1. **Acceptance:** You have to *accept* what you know about the world as it really is, not who you wish it—or even yourself—to be.

2. **Action:** Once you accept and know the world, and the game, for what it is, you can *act* appropriately with a positive, active response (as opposed to a negative response, which we'll cover shortly).

We think you will find that once you can accept the way the world is—and not the way you want it to be—and act on that information appropriately, you will be able to respond more quickly, more naturally, and more personally *when it matters most.*

The Acceptance-Action Response

The Acceptance-Action Response is a two-part exercise to stabilize your emotional baseline. First, you must learn to *accept* the situation for what it is, not how it should be in an "ideal" world.

Game play is much different from practice, and tournament play can be even more challenging than regular match play. What happens with your coach in a practice match is not always how it will play out in a tournament or competitive match.

In fact, it rarely is. Arguing about it or letting your emotions get the best of you will only make things worse; accept the current situation and "play the ball as it bounces."

The second part of the Acceptance-Action Response is to *act*—act on the information you have, not some dream game you're playing in your head. If you get a bad bounce, and you decide to kill it anyway, watching it sail off to the left when you expected to nail it on the right, that is neither accepting nor acting; that is failing. You must accept *and* act to find the baseline that is right for you.

This chapter will help you become more familiar with the Acceptance-Action Response and begin to use it more often in your daily life.

Step 1: Acceptance

In the chapter "Experience," we talked specifically about how to handle the experiences that come your way on and off the court. We learned that life isn't always what you want it to be, and that the only way to face the future was to embrace the future—as it comes, as it is.

In this chapter we are talking more about getting to know yourself, what you're good at, your strengths, and your weaknesses, because the more you know about yourself, the easier it is to accept the way the world is.

Before you act, you must accept. Before you accept, you must know.

Why is acceptance so important? Simple: *You can only have a really positive action response if you accept what just happened.* If you deny what you see around you—how the ball is bouncing, how well your opponent is playing, what the weather is like, how well you're responding to the match's little surprises—then you won't truly be able to respond appropriately.

There are two ways to respond to any event:

1. **Acceptance:** You can accept what the event is and deal with it from that basis.

2. **Denial:** You can deny what you see, feel, and hear and approach the event that way.

Of the two responses, most of us can agree that denial is the easiest route to take. Oddly enough, denial happens a lot in tennis. You play someone you think is "not that good," but suddenly he or she is hitting some great shots.

"Lucky shot," you mumble, "but it will pass. This guy/gal's not that good."

So since you're in denial, you don't react to what's really happening. You don't change anything about, or with, your game. You just keep thinking, shot after shot, "It will pass and he/she will start missing again," without having any action response to the real situation.

Many matches get lost by this habit, and in this example you can see how denial makes you slow to adjust to the reality of what's happening around you.

On the other hand, if you accept the game for what it is and assess the situation with a realistic, logical, and unemotional outlook, you can act more appropriately—and win more often.

Accepting Your Emotions

Every event, whether positive or negative, creates emotions inside you. Fear, doubt, insecurity, anxiety, anger, pride, joy, confidence, and trust—all these emotions are common on the tennis court. But if you don't deal with them, if you don't accept them for what they are and move on from there, you can't have an appropriate action response to help you move forward.

The main thing is to be honest about yourself and how you feel right now, in the moment. Forget how you want to feel or how you should feel. Instead, respect how you actually feel and what's physically happening at the moment. Also, be honest about how you feel about your opponent.

To accept anything, you have to expect everything. In other words, you have to put your preconceived notions on hold and play the cards you're dealt. You can't control everything—your opponent, the weather, the court conditions, even the line judge—but you can control your own action and response. When it comes to acceptance, it's important to focus on what you can control.

As Michael Jordan once said, "One thing I learned from my father was that he taught me to always take responsibility for things I can control but not to take responsibility for things that I couldn't."[1]

Don't waste time responding to, fretting over, or even acting on things you can't control. Instead, focus your energies and enthusiasm for things you can control, such as

- your stamina;
- your endurance;

1   Sam Smith, *The Jordan Rules* (New York: Pocket Books, 1993)

- the amount of rest you've had before a match;
- your state of mind;
- your acceptance of the game as it is;
- your action response;
- the way you prepare for the match.

And what about your opponent? You will never be able to control him or her, so why even try? Spend your time on controlling your game, your actions, and your responses instead.

Let's say your opponent is acing you through the middle of the court most of the time. What can you do about this? You can deny it and hope he or she will start missing. Or you can take action by covering the center of the court a bit more, but you can't control the fact that he or she is sending the ball 125 miles per hour close to the line!

Pro players accept the speed and placement and focus on where they can influence their game, such as shortening their stroke to have more time or moving to block the serve, where lesser-experienced players play the victim, telling the world how this "lucky person" can hit such a ball time and again. While it's easier to make this kind of denial, this blame game, it only blocks them from finding solutions.

You have to accept before you act; then it can lead to a good action and, more importantly, a good action response.

Honesty Leads to Acceptance

You have to be honest with your emotions and accept the way you feel. Take fear, for example. Many players think they need to be brave and fight the feelings of fear they may have when approaching a seemingly superior player, a big tournament, a new court, or whatever.

From our experience on the tour, we have never met a player who has honestly said he or she never felt fear or insecurity, including number-one players in the world on the ATP and WTA tours.

The thing about fear is that it exists, and it will always exist—for you, for us, and for every player. It's human nature; we're hardwired to be aware of fear, experience it, and respond to it. What happens with some players, though, is that they feel the fear and deny it, thinking that will make them stronger, braver, better players (or that it will go away if they don't pay attention to it). It doesn't; it only makes them weaker.

Let's say you're playing for break point and you're afraid it's the last one in the match. That may or may not be true, but the more pressure—or fear—you put on yourself, the less effective you'll be as a player. You have to do what you can—emotions are not absolute. You might feel a little scared, or very scared. You might feel very sure of yourself, or kind of sure. The key is to listen to your inner self and do what you can do in this moment. If you feel a bit insecure, take a bit of the edge off your placement or speed. No need to step back a lot if you feel it lightly. If the emotion is stronger, a bigger change might be appropriate.

As Rafael Nadal once said, "Fear is not my enemy; fear of losing is my enemy."[2] Or Michael Jordan, who has been quoted as saying, "I never looked at the consequences of missing a big shot... when you think about the consequences you always think of a negative result."[3]

Take serving, for instance. In the beginning of a match, when the scoreboard is clean and you have a little room for error, your fear may be less because if you fault, even double-fault, you can still make that up later in the match.

But as the match progresses and the score gets closer and there is not as much wriggle room, players can become paralyzed with fear over double-faulting. We were listening to a top-ranked player talk to her coach after winning a big tournament and she said, "I was so afraid of committing a double fault on that set point, I almost couldn't serve!"

This fear happens to us all, but the key is to *overcome it*. This player knew that fear could paralyze her if she let it, but she didn't. She played through (she accepted the fear and did what she could) and won the match. So if top players have emotional

---

2   www.tennispsychology.com.

3   www.mindtraining.net.

problems just like the rest of us, chances are you will have them to. Just like the game's top players, chances are you too will

- get scared;
- get insecure;
- have doubt;
- get emotional;
- miss an open shot once in a while;
- experience that your weaker points might get weaker;
- experience that your strongest point might not work.

But just like the game's top players, chances are you too will

- feel safe and confident on one of your "lesser strokes";
- feel emotional or rock solid;
- stay calm in very stressful situations;
- feel brave and positively aggressive;
- make a shot that you normally don't make.

The key thing here is to listen to your feelings and act on them, good or bad. Now that you know such things will happen at some point, the best you can do is be prepared. Being prepared means you have to have a plan—or a strategy—to handle these moments. As a useful strategy, we use a tool we got from one of our colleagues, Bane Bradonic. This is just a small part of his mental programs.

The key thing is to be clear on your own abilities under pressure. Know yourself, be honest with yourself, and you will find out what actions are most likely to work for you, because they have worked for you in the past and are based on your personality.

Track Your Fifty Successes

It's easy to put on a show when there is no pressure, but when players are competing and under immense pressure, who they are—at the core of their being—can't really hide.

The Fifty Successes exercise is something we do with our students to discover what works for them under pressure by creating their own personal strategy to succeed in these situations.

This is a great exercise that anybody can do at any time. What we have students do is take a few weeks and write down what we call their "fifty success stories." These can be anything they've achieved; they don't have to be tennis related. The main thing to remember before adding something to your "Fifty Successes" list is that it has felt like a success, something you felt proud to achieve.

Now, don't rush. It takes a surprising amount of time to come up with your Fifty Successes, so give yourself at least three to five weeks to fill up the list. Once you've completed your original list of fifty, look at it again and create a top-ten list from that first fifty.

What we often see in these Fifty Successes lists is a theme that shines through. You'll read five, ten, fifteen, maybe twenty or twenty-five success stories these players have had and they all revolve around some key skills they possess, such as

- persevering through pain;
- fighting back after a loss;
- being brave and taking chances;
- being creative;
- being consistent;
- having great tactical skills;
- being mentally tough.

So as you complete this exercise, be on high alert for themes that come to light, maybe things you weren't even aware of about yourself. Let's say you see a few successes that prove you have mental toughness. You can work with that! It's all about expectation. If you reach a tough point in the match, you have to know—and expect—what you are capable of under pressure. If your key thing is that you are creative under pressure in most of your Fifty Successes, then that's what you have to do under pressure—get creative!

Expect to be creative, take action, and create something. If your key point is that you are tough, expect yourself to be tough. If your Fifty Successes are reached because you play tactical, that's great. Expect to play a very tactical, smart point. This gets you in the habit of building on your successes, finding your courage, and expecting to succeed because you know your strengths.

If you and all the people in your inner circle are on the same page, everybody knows what to expect from you under pressure—and **what** you do, is something that you **can** do under pressure.

A top player can't have anyone important expect something of him or her that he or she can't do under pressure. A common mistake of less self-aware players is that they can do things in practice or in no-pressure situations, but if it is not linked to the core of your personality, chances are it will crack under pressure. And this will lead to frustration.

As coaches, we can use these Fifty Successes to remind players of what they've accomplished in the past and encourage them to do so in the future.

Use the form below to list your favorite Fifty Successes.

Write down your successes, and then after each one, describe why you felt it was important.

My Fifty Successes in Life (So Far):

Describe your successes and why they felt important.

1. _____
2. _____
3. _____
4. _____
5. _____
6. _____
7. _____
8. _____
9. _____
10. _____
11. _____
12. _____
13. _____
14. _____
15. _____
16. _____
17. _____
18. _____
19. _____
20. _____
21. _____
22. _____
23. _____
24. _____

25. _____
26. _____
27. _____
28. _____
29. _____
30. _____
31. _____
32. _____
33. _____
34. _____
35. _____
36. _____
37. _____
38. _____
39. _____
40. _____
41. _____
42. _____
43. _____
44. _____
45. _____
46. _____
47. _____
48. _____
49. _____
50. _____

What is your form telling you? What have you learned about yourself from this exercise? We like to have our players use a yellow or green highlighter and go through their list, finding traits that match or success stories that really "pop" and creating a top-ten list of their biggest successes.

Now, choose the biggest successes from the top-fifty list (in your opinion) and write after them what "skill" you think was at the base of these successes:

My Top-Ten Successes

1. _____
2. _____
3. _____
4. _____
5. _____
6. _____
7. _____
8. _____
9. _____
10. _____

Step 2: Action Response

When the pressure is on, the basic mindset of a Pro player is "I will throw the best thing I have at you, and you have to be pretty good to handle this."

Respond with Action

Why is it so important to know your strengths, your personality, and your road to success? Simply because you have to be ready to respond right after every point; this is known as your action response.

After a good point, most pro players have either a calm or no response or a positive active response. So you will see things like

- sidestepping right after the point;
- a clenched fist;
- punching the air;
- verbally cheering themselves on;
- tapping themselves on the leg or shoe.

These are *active responses*, underlining that they did well.

After losing a point, we see many differences in inexperienced player's active response! For instance, players might

- curse or shout;
- throw their racket;
- hit themselves in the head with their racquet;
- stomp their feet;
- yell at themselves.

So the active response is a sort of order you give to yourself that you will follow up in the next point, things like:

- "Be aggressive"
- "Move in."
- "Spin it."
- "Keep it simple."
- "Step in on the return."
- "Stick to the plan."

So in the first two seconds after a point there will be a response—good or bad. There is a big difference between future matches, challenger matches, and ATP and WTA matches. The difference is what you hear and see.

In future matches, for instance, you will often hear things like this a lot:

- "Wow, this is so bad."
- "F**k!"
- "Such a bad shot."
- "That's the third time in a row I missed this shot!"
- "Man, what a lucky shot."
- "I just can't serve today."
- "F**king this" or "F**king that."

And you might see things like this:

- a negative facial reactions of disgust
- throwing or bouncing the racquet
- smashing the ball into the fence

Just like in the positive side, these responses underline what just happened, emphasizing the negative. These responses are judgments of you or your opponent. They are referring to the past (minutes, hours, or sometimes even years):

- "Why do I always miss the ball?"
- "Why is he/she always better than me?"
- "How come I can never win against him/her?"
- "Why can't I ever return his/her serve?"

Many players in lower-rated tournaments do this a lot. "Trash-talking yourself" still happens once in a while in pro matches on the tour, but the higher you go, the less it occurs. Pro players know that emphasizing unsuccessful points does not help.

A nonverbal response can also accompany a verbal response. For instance, a player might miss a shot because he or she is slow to move his or her feet and say to himself or herself, "Come on, move it!" Even though he or she missed the shot, his or her action response is still appropriate because he or she is responding actively. In other words, the player is underlining what he or she has to do: "move faster."

Less professional or inexperienced players might respond with a judgment or negative self-feedback or even a question, like, "What is wrong with you? You move like a turtle!"

Judgment responses are rarely helpful because rather than solving a problem, they simply make it worse by adding aggravation, stress, anxiety, and insecurity to your game.

The Action Response in Picture Form

In the figure below, you will see the action response brought to life:

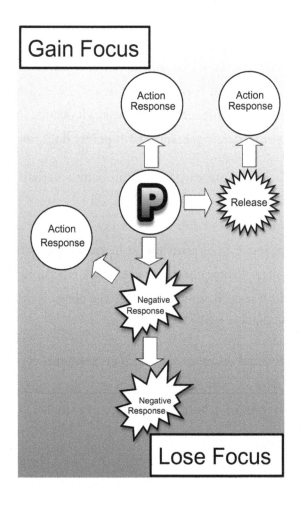

The circle "P" in the middle of our diagram stands for "the point played." You can see arrows pointing away from the point played in a generally "up" or "down" movement. This refers to the action response a player can make directly after a point has been played, won or lost.

In this case, the player has three kinds of responses he or she can make:

1. An action response
2. Release
3. A negative response

If you look at the direction of the arrows, a negative response always brings you down. Cursing yourself, judging yourself, bringing up the past, getting emotional to no positive result—these are all negative responses that bring you further and further away from effective game play. Being negative on yourself because you realize you responding negatively will get you down even more.

There is also something known as "the release." Also known as blowing off steam (such as maybe a short scream), this is something that happens in passionate matches. If this is your action response to a shot, no problem—just let it go. If you follow these releases up with a good action response, you're right back on track.

The best type of action response is *something you can do*—a movement, a statement, a reaction, a motion that gets you moving in the right direction.

It's real, it's positive, it's forward, and it's in the moment. It's not something you wish would happen or want to happen, but it's something you can physically or mentally do to keep yourself playing professionally.

Examples of a positive action response are things like,

- "Okay, move."
- "Hit it."
- "Keep swinging."
- "Go to the net."
- "Hit it crosscourt."

While gruff and occasionally heated, these responses are appropriate because they mean you are adapting, growing, responding positively, and focusing more on actions.

Rather than discouraging great game play, these responses are actually encouraging you to move on. You don't necessarily have to say these things out loud, but you can think them and they'll be just as effective.

The So-Called Easy Shot

One of the most negative "responses" you can have during a match is saying something like, "How could you miss that? It was such an easy shot!"

Often you don't even have to tell yourself that; your inner circle will respond in that way, or even the fans in the stands! But was it really an easy shot? Let's look closer to see.

The difference between an "easy" shot and a "hard" one is often how you feel about it! What looks "easy" from outside the court can often be quite difficult to the player on the court.

Pro players know that if some thought, fear, or other distraction comes into your mind in a split second, the level of difficulty shoots up. That's the level of difficulty you are facing. *Deny this, and you feel like you screw up; accept it, and you are challenged.*

Resulting in thoughts like: "Wow, this was so stupid. I should have won it easily. How could I miss that easy shot?" The basic idea is, all these things happen to all top-ten players a few times in a year.

They don't make a big deal out of it. They know exactly what happened point by point while taking their thought and the mental level of difficulty into account and will try to deal with it in the next moment. But it's not only about the so-called easy shot. There are many situations when inexperienced players think they are "easy" when, in fact, they are not. They feel stupid that these things happen to them, getting down on themselves and thinking things like,

- "You won the first set 6-3 and were 3–1 up in the second set and still lost."
- "You were serving for the match and got broken."
- "You broke your opponent and got broken right back."
- "You are 5–4 up and 40–0 on the serve of the opponent."
- "You won the first set 6–0 and lost the second set 1–6."

These are the typical reactions of inexperienced players. Pro players know these things do happen a lot, so it is not something you "messed up." Pro players approach these things differently. They know that three match points is an opportunity, but not really if your opponent aces you three times.

They know that to close out a match serving still means you have to play a good game against a big fighting opponent. In all these situations, pro players measure what happened by seeing and feeling what they did in relation to what the opponent was throwing at them at that moment, and what they were able to do with this.

Tennis is hard and pro players make it look easy. Meanwhile, they know for sure it is hard, but that's no reason to stress yourself out. Hard or easy, every shot deserves a strong action response following it.

Then too, your personal definition of "easy" depends on the situation and skill level as much as on the thought and feeling you might have. Don't make the mistake of judging a shot's difficulty purely on the skill needed. Face your thoughts and feelings and deal with the whole picture.

Practice Level Versus Match Level

In any given match, anything can happen. Remember this truism as you move forward in your play. There are practice levels of play, where you exist in a controlled environment, always know your opponent—a coach, pal, or sparring player—and can generally expect the same thing to happen time and time again. Then there is competitive or match-level play, where anything can happen—any match, anytime!

Pro players don't get trapped into thinking their practice level can be compared to the match level of an opponent they might have seen play a few weeks ago. Pro players know that practice matches are just practice. Dealing with an important match situation changes everything. So all expectations should be off, and let's see who deals with the situation best today.

Know Your Opponent

You're not alone in this battle. Often we get so emotional about a match, so fearful or anxious or frustrated, that we think we're the only ones on the court. We're not.

Many players on the junior or future level stop looking over the net when they get negative or emotional. This way they don't really realize if the opponent also might be struggling physically or emotionally. Seeing your opponent struggle also makes it more of a competition over who can control his or her situation first.

Know your opponent and try to get a sense of what he or she is going through. Can you sense him or her breaking down? Taking it slow? Losing control? Is he or she in much better shape than you saw him or her in last time you played? Or worse shape?

Your opponent is a variable that is constantly shifting, morphing, and evolving. You can't just keep your eye on the ball; you must constantly watch, analyze, process, and predict your opponent as well!

Chapter 3: Respect

Respect is one of the core values we teach all of our students, from the least experienced to the most, from junior players to our ATP and WTA pros. Specifically, to succeed you must respect your *opponents*, respect your *surroundings*, and, above all, respect *yourself*.

You can't ever get overconfident by thinking you are superior to another player simply because you have a higher ranking than he or she does.

For instance, just because a player has a lower rank than you today, it doesn't mean he or she will play a less accomplished game than you. If anything, he or she may even be "hungrier" than you are and play a harder, more accomplished game!

If you ever watch Roger Federer play against his opponents, no matter where they are ranked, he always approaches them as if this could be the time he is upset; he always gives them much respect on and off the court.

The Three Types of Respect

While respect itself is a fundamental value all tennis players should learn, there are actually three types of respect we should be concerned with on and off the court:

1. **Respect for your opponent**: Who is your opponent? What are his or her strengths? What are his or her weaknesses? How can you best assess his or her play without disrespecting him or her as a player? When you respect your opponent enough to see his or her skills objectively, you can keep your focus where it belongs: on the game and not on your perception of whether the other player is a "good" or "bad" person.

2. **Respect for your surroundings**: What tournament are you in? What city or state? Who is sponsoring the tournament? Who is the line judge? The opponent's coach? The opponent's trainer? It's very easy to come into a smaller tournament and complain about such things as an inexperienced line judge, the hotel, the ball kids, the practice courts, etc. But the fact remains, only you can win or lose the match. (You signed up for the tournament. You decided to put

yourself there.) Check where you go before, adjust your expectations, and deal with it. Disrespecting your surroundings takes the focus off the one person who can make a difference in your play: yourself. Wherever you are, whatever the conditions, whoever is on staff or judging on the line, the focus should always be on yourself.

3. **Respect for yourself**: Finally, what about you? Do you respect yourself? We often think, of course, that we respect ourselves, but as coaches we hear a lot of negative self-talk on the circuit, and every time you dredge up the past, call yourself names like "loser," "weak," "worthless," or even "stupid," "f**ing idiot," or "a**s h**e," you are disrespecting yourself.

Respect = Control

More than anything, *respect is a feeling*. Whether you disrespect an opponent, your surroundings, or yourself out loud or just in your head, you can't hide your feelings from yourself. And what we know about feelings is that you can't hide from them on the court, either.

What you feel will always come out when you least expect it.

When you feel respect, your emotions are balanced. You are, as they say, calm, cool, and collected. You're not hating on your opponent or feeling too big for the tournament. You're not feeling prideful, rude, superior, judgmental, or cocky, and so your emotions—and thus your emotional baseline—will be balanced and you'll be able to play at your best.

However, if you feel disrespect in your heart—whether you verbalize it or not—you will feel emotionally unbalanced and it will affect your play, consciously or subconsciously. That's why it's critical not to just fake respect but to genuinely feel it, sincerely, in your heart—respect for your opponent, for your surroundings, and particularly for yourself.

Ultimately, respect is about control—controlling your emotions and not giving in to petty name-calling. Like so many of the lessons in this book, the more control you have, the closer you are to a professional "baseline".

Controlling your responses, both verbal and nonverbal, is a good first step. In the short term, having more control on the court will help you be a more focused, balanced player. That's the short-term, "see it happen today" goal. But real change— and real balance—comes only when you really respect yourself enough to make these changes stick, on and off the court.

Next we will talk about how to respect both yourself and your opponent, on and off the court—how not to do it, how to do it, and, perhaps most importantly, *why* to do it.

What You Say about Others Reflects Back on You

There is a big difference in the way inexperienced players and professional players communicate, with each other and with themselves. Inexperienced players tend to

- **Blame others when they lose, miss a shot, etc.**
    - *"The guy's a top seed. What chance do I have?"*
    - *"What a crappy court. There is not one normal bounce!"*

- **Victimize themselves**
    - *"The line judge hates me. The fans hate me. I don't have a chance. I'll never win here."*

- **Take credit for wins they didn't necessarily earn**
    - *"That match was so easy, we shouldn't even have been on the same court together."*
    - *"I won 6–4 in the third; I fell asleep in the second."*

- **Be arrogant and disrespectful**
    - *"This player's a loser!"*
    - *"This guy has no backhand."*
    - *"He is a pusher. That's not tennis."*
    - *"This tournament's lame!"*

- ◦ *"If I hit two balls in the court, I win this match easily."*

- **Dwell in the past**
  - ◦ *"I beat him soundly last tournament, so this match should be a breeze."*
  - ◦ *"I've never lost against her. She can't beat me."*

- **Focus on the future**
  - ◦ *"I was off my game today. I'll nail him next tournament!"*

- **Ignore the present**
  - ◦ *"This guy's having a great day and I feel lousy. No wonder he's winning!"*
  - ◦ *"The guy plays like he is dreaming—he's so lucky!"*

More experienced, professional players tend to

- **Respect others regardless of their reputation**
  - ◦ *"I know he can have a bad temper, but I have to be prepared in case he stays in control today. He's really competitive when he's focused."*

- **Give respect to their opponent**
  - ◦ *"Man, this guy's pretty good. I'll have to bring my A-game today."*

- "I know this guy's ranked lower than I am, but I still have to be careful because he's been strong in his last few matches."

- **Take credit when credit is due**
    - "I played a good game today and am proud that I won."
    - "Hey, I was tough. I kept my focus for the whole match."

- **Ignore the past**
    - "I've beaten her soundly in the last three tournaments, but I hear she's with a new coach now and has been really working on her strength training, so I need to stay on my toes."

- **Prepare the future**
    - "I've never played this opponent on a clay court before, so I'm eager to see how this plays out."

- **Focus on the present**
    - "Okay, now that I know his backhand is strong, I'll focus on his forehand and see if that strategy works."

If you look at the two kinds of statements closely, you'll see that the main difference between them is simply *respect*. Making snap judgments ("This guy looks like a clown," "His coach is young and inexperienced") or calling names or dissing an opponent over something like his or her reputation ("He's a hothead," "She's lazy") or his or her appearance ("fat," "slow," "weak") can be big mistakes when you find yourself outmatched because you underestimated your opponent—and overestimated yourself.

It's a very clear equation that leads to focus and balance: when you *give respect*, you *gain control*—and a proper perspective that's unclouded by reputation or rash judgments. For example, if you ask a pro player about his opponent's forehand versus his backhand, you might hear something fairly calm and logical like this: "Well, his forehand is probably stronger than his backhand, so if you pressure his backhand, you can probably find some opportunities to force points that might not occur with another player."

In this case, the focus isn't so much on disrespecting the player with terms like "bad" or "weak" but on how to respect the opponent's play and also find opportunities for yourself to match it and, hopefully, prevail over it.

A less experienced player, when asked the same question, might say something like, "You can't lose against this clown because his backhand is so weak you just hit to that every time, easy." This kind of disrespect for another player can be very detrimental to you, because what if this player has been working on his backhand? Or what if it isn't so weak after all?

Or your forehand isn't so strong? Being overconfident is a direct result of simply not respecting your opponent's strengths and weaknesses.

Inexperienced players will often say the following things when talking about other players:

- "This guy has no backhand."
- "He's weak; he can't kill the ball."
- "The guy just pushes everything back. He's barely playing tennis."
- "The guy is a loose cannon, no control whatsoever."
- "He will hit it in the fence."
- "She plays with her eyes closed."
- "She is too fat to move."
- "She is a choker. When it's tight, she will screw it up."
- "She can't serve."
- "Look what she's wearing. It's a joke!"

These types of statements are not only disrespectful to your opponent, but they cheapen the competitive experience by taking whatever skills these opponents *do* have off the court— and out of the equation—completely.

What's worse, they're often inaccurate. Take the statement, "She's too fat to move." We often hear this said about larger players. Clearly, it's a simple and quick statement to undermine that player's value, but it can really come back to the person who says it, because just as often, larger players have true power behind the ball and can really surprise you!

Now, let's take a look at what inexperienced players often say to each other:

- *"I gave her a tennis lesson (by beating her so badly)."*
    - It is never respectful to imply that you taught another player something simply because you won a match. Many things go into your win and another player's loss. And next time, if you're not careful and get too cocky, he or she could be giving you a tennis lesson instead. If you think winning with clear numbers is "giving a lesson," that probably exaggerates the level difference between you and your opponent. Clearly, your opponent is not in the same league as you. But it also means that if you lose against someone with big numbers, you also think someone has been "teaching" you a lesson, and you are not even in the same league with your opponent. So by being cocky in the past, or going down on your opponent big time, you automatically will put yourself down more when you lose in big numbers.

- *"This guy I played today, he never played this well in his whole life."*
  - Here we see an inexperienced player placing the blame on someone other than himself. True, your opponent may have played better than ever, but an experienced player would have been ready for that by respecting his or her opponent in the first place. That's not to say an experienced player would have won that match anyway, but he or she would have been ready to make it tougher at any moment, as even the slightest drop in level of this good playing opponent. Inexperienced players get a bit too caught up in their "why this is happening to me" thinking, causing them to miss out on these little moments of opportunity to turn the match.

- *"I beat her 6–2 and 6–2 last week. She should be no problem for you."*
  - You can't apply one match to another, one player to another, or even one day to the next. Let the other player judge for himself or herself how he or she should play this opponent, and don't judge others too quickly—or harshly—based on one isolated bit of "evidence." Pro players know that every day, every moment, is different. Prepare yourself for what you

have to do to win, and be ready to adjust to anything that might turn out to be different today.

- *"I lost last week but should have won easily."*
  - ° If you should have won easily, why didn't you? Actually, we teach our players that "should have" does not exist. You played the match, and you were not able to find the solutions to play a winning level on this day, in this situation. There is no "should have," only what happened. The solution is to be better prepared, have more respect, and play better next time.

- *"He was so lucky. Everything fell on the line for him."*
  - ° Again, be careful of blaming others or excusing your own poor play on an opponent's "luck" or you're just having "a bad day." Don't victimize yourself. Focus on the things you could have done and try to be on top of every opportunity next time. And, by the way, well played to your opponent.

- *"He stole that match from me. For sure that break point was in."*
  - Here you are playing "the blame game" again. For sure we know this much: no one ever wins the blame game. On lower level tournaments, more matches get lost by the aggravation following the discussion, than by the actual missed call. So the old adage really does apply: *Don't get mad, get even!* In other words, focus on playing really well, not on stealing back.

- *"I lost 6–1 to her, but it should have been 6–1 for me."*
  - Well, if it should have been, why wasn't it?

- *"I beat this girl easily in 2 sets (7–5 and 7–6)."*
  - Define "easy." Your easy might not be another player's easy, and vice versa. Listening to these kinds of remarks always gives us the idea that this player might be losing the grip on reality here.

7–5 and 7–6 is not "easy," and 1–6 could not "easily" have been the other way around!

When you say these things to other players, you do them a disservice, because you aren't giving them all the information at your disposal. It's like you're self-editing before you speak.

Often these statements are made in retrospect, or in passing, without a lot of thought or providing all the details.

Maybe by now (a few days or a few weeks later) it seems "easy" to have beaten that opponent in two sets (7–5 and 7–6), but perhaps it didn't seem so easy at the time and, frankly, that's far from a rout.

Our lesson is to avoid saying disrespectful things about other players, and, what's more, not to listen to them either. They don't do anyone any good, and the more you believe them, the more they will come back to bite you when it's your time to play this opponent you've been so disrespectful about—or some other opponent you may have disrespected or taken for granted.

Let's combine what you've read so far when it comes to respect and disrespect. The real rules of the game? The real rules of tennis state the following:

- The sun will get in your eyes.
- The rain will make the court dangerous.
- The wind will influence the direction of the ball.
- Balls will bounce badly.
- Crowds will be noisy.
- Line judges will be less than perfect.
- Strings will break.
- The ball will hit the net.
- Competitors will (usually) be (a lot) stronger/smarter than you thought!

So, with these realities in mind, the law of averages states that you will be behind in some matches because of a combination of the above "rules." Experienced players know this and adjust their play accordingly. If a string breaks, they don't blame Wilson or Babolat. They simply grab a new racket and get back on the court.

You can choose respect and control over disrespect and chaos. You can choose to blame others or control yourself. Ultimately, it's your choice to be behind the fat girl in the funny dress who is so lucky today that all her balls are falling on the line. Or you can choose to be behind the hard-hitting girl who is playing close to the line. We think this second choice will make it a lot easier to stay competitive and strong. The game is difficult enough. Adding disrespect to the equation is not helping you to get into the state of finding solutions fast.

How to Talk to Yourself Respectfully

There is a difference in how less experienced players talk to themselves and how the pros talk to themselves, and the main difference is something we like to call *awareness*.

For example, a less experienced player might be facing an opponent he or she has played and won against six times in the past and say, "I can't lose against this player. There's just no way." In the same situation, a pro player might approach a game in which he or she has beaten the same opponent six previous times and say, "If all goes like the last several matches, I *should* win, but I still need to be aware that this player been in training for the last six months and has a wicked backhand that gave me trouble last time."

Again, respect often comes down to awareness, in this case self-awareness. Rather than dwelling on how weak the competition is or how small the tournament may be or who's coaching whom, instead be concerned about your own game, your own strengths, and your own weaknesses, and how they relate directly to your opponent. If you start with disrespecting your opponent first and then factor yourself in, you're focusing on the wrong awareness—and definitely in the wrong order.

Here are some very common things we hear players say to themselves all the time:

- *"I am stupid."*
- *"I am too slow."*
- *"I am too bad. Why don't I just quit tennis?"*
- *"I am so stupid. How could I have missed that ball?"*
- *"I am not hitting one single forehand into the court today."*

These kinds of negative self-talk make you disrespect yourself more than anyone else. Words have power, and enough negative words said about yourself can have truly negative repercussions during actual game play, when they become self-fulfilling prophecies instead of just negative self-talk. Learn to respect yourself and you will respect your game that much more. Not to mention, most of us don't exactly "whisper" such things when we say them aloud in the "heat of the battle." (In fact, quite the opposite is usually true.) As a gentle reminder, your opponents can usually hear this "self-talk" and adjust their game accordingly!

When you speak ill of yourself, basically disrespecting yourself on the court, you are doing a bad job of coaching yourself. Focusing on only the negatives takes the emphasis off your many positives.

Dwelling in the past, letting one bad shot ruin the whole match, or basically calling yourself disrespectful names like "loser," "weak," and "idiot" will shift your focus away from winning and straight to losing.

Experienced players, especially the most successful ones, are good "self-coaches." They know to live in the moment and to not dwell on the past or even get too anxious about the future, but instead to play point by point based on the evidence in front of them in the moment.

So, we've seen how not to talk to yourself on the court, but how should you talk? Imagine if a good friend were speaking to you about the game in progress—not yesterday's game, not tomorrow's game, but this game, right now, and how you're doing in the moment. That's the kind of good coach/good friend you should be to yourself:

- supportive
- helpful
- focused
- thoughtful
- honest

While we'll talk about your coaches, your friends, your parents, and your "inner circle" a little later in this chapter, we all know that the "coach" you spend the most time with is yourself. Be the best self-coach you can be, on and off the court.

How Being Disrespectful Costs You

In an average match, depending on the fluctuation of scoring and competitive play, there are 120 to 250 points played. Every point makes a difference.

If you study the points after a match very closely, you can see that not only does every point count, but matches can be won or lost by just a few points. The good news is that we can help. All these little things we talk about in the book will make you a bit more stable when it comes to your game. And being a bit more emotionally balanced here and there might lead to dropping less points here and there.

It's a war of averages. The more balanced, focused, and stable you are every game, the fewer points you lose. It's not necessarily winning every match every time, but winning more points, in more games, more often.

Pro players know that most matches are decided with just a few points' difference between winning and losing. Five points, more or less, can make the difference between 6–3, 6–4 and 3–6, 4–6.

Have a Functioning Inner Circle

Who you spend time with is just as important as what you do with your time. There is a saying that says, "You are who your ten best friends are." In other words, the people you spend the most time with will ultimately influence you for better or worse.

We call those people who have the most influence on you as a player and a person your "inner circle." Some inner circles are small; maybe you are only really close with two or three people. Other inner circles are quite large, with as many as ten to fifteen people. It's a very personal thing, this inner circle. Regardless of how big or small it is, your inner circle includes people like

- your coaches;
- your trainers;
- your parents;

- your teammates;
- your friends.

Obviously, the inner circle is very important to the player, because they have a significant impact on and off the court. So if you are part of that inner circle, please pay particular attention to this chapter, because soon you will fully realize just how big of an impact you can make on the emotional stability of the tennis player.

For coaches, fellow players, mentors, parents, other family members, and friends who may be part of the player's inner circle, trust is an extremely important issue. The more a player trusts you, the more important it is to say the right things, share the right values, and even share the right messages.

As coaches, we are definitely aware of how much of an influence we have on our players. Are you? If you're part of a player's circle of influence, handle that player—and how you interact with him or her—with care.

Beware of "False Information"

Oftentimes, we can receive pieces of "false information" from our inner circle. They can have opinions and attitudes that aren't exactly respectful or, for that matter, helpful to your growth as a player. Here are some pieces of "false information" it might be better to avoid:

- *"Hit that old player of the court."*
  - ° In this case, "old" might be just a few years older than you! And quite often, older players are wiser ones, who know better than to let their emotions get the best of them. Pro players know that anyone can press out his or her top level for one day, but that he or she might not be able to play like that the whole year. But be ready. This day might be today.

- *"Come on; this person is seeded/high-ranked/one year older. You have nothing to lose."*
  - ° Telling a player he or she has nothing to lose sets him or her up to do just that: lose. We have seen players get very angry at a person who said this. Sure, they want to help you or make you feel good. But if you are not seeded in a big tournament, you are probably seeded in the smaller tournament next week. So you just also implied to the player that he or her has everything to prove—and everything to lose—next week.

- *"You are such great player/you are so talented/you can win this tournament."*
    - These statements may all be true, but are they true today? Whoever says these things probably wants to build up confidence. But if you are 1–4 down against somebody with a lower ranking in the first round, you might feel the urge to show your friends that they are right, because they believe you are so great, when all you need to do right now is to get back on earth and maybe just get down and fight to survive.

- *"Your opponent lost first round in the last few tournaments."*
    - This kind of statement puts you at all kinds of odds. First, it sets you up for disappointment if he or she doesn't lose the first round in this tournament. Second, it makes you question your skills if you can't beat him or her. Third, losing three times in a row does not mean it's going to be easy or the opponent won't play his or her best today. If anything, this statement can only make you unprepared.

- *"Your opponent only played one good tournament last year."*
    - ° Last year isn't just the past—it's a long way in the past. A lot can happen in a year. So what are you implying, he or she will not play good today? Or, if he or she is playing good today, you are very unlucky since this happens only one time a year? A pro player would say, "So if he played one good tournament last year, for sure he can play. I better take my time and figure out how to play him."

- *"This player is getting old."*
    - ° Making these kind of disparaging remarks about your opponents only lessens the amount of respect you give them during actual play, where it really counts—and "old," "young," "slow", "skinny", "fat," or whatever players might just surprise you. Again, really understanding the pro game means asking better questions: "He is getting old? What does that mean, he is slower? Or so experienced that he sees earlier where you are hitting? Less powerful? Or so experienced not to make any mistakes in placement?" Again, do not let these kinds of

remarks make you unprepared for whatever competition you may face.

- *"You always play well in this tournament."*
  - ° Even if it's a positive statement, living in the past—or the future—is no good way to stay focused on the present. It might be a nice feeling to walk on the court like this. Just don't let it lure you into the comfort zone too much where you lose your edge. Pro players know, every series has an end—every. By the way, by making the thought (I always play well on this tournament) stronger on some tournaments, you will also strengthen the idea that you never play well on some other tournaments.

- *"This player is a jerk. Teach this player a lesson."*
  - ° Making judgments about what "type" of a person your opponent is merely takes your focus away from what kind of player he or she is. Making a fight too personal will distract you from choosing the best solution, because you are following another goal in the back of your mind. For example, you might go for a body shot where a passing shot would have been more efficient.

- *"This match is no problem for you. You are playing good at the moment, and she is not so good."*
  - This type of false information can give you the idea that you don't have to work for it anymore. Pros know that to play good in the morning does not mean you will play good in the afternoon. Again, stay in the moment and react to it *in* the moment—and *only* in the moment.

- *"I saw the schedule. If you win the first match, the draw is wide-open."*
  - When you hear something like this, you are already thinking ahead to the future, losing the focus on winning the actual game you're playing. Saying this to a pro is a big irritation. Pro players know that you can't "talk your way" into the final. You have to respect and play every opponent in that given moment.

The harm in these statements isn't necessarily that someone you trust in your inner circle is saying them but that you believe them. When you believe such disrespectful statements, or you start to believe their sometimes-unrealistic expectations of your skills, you cloud your judgment and begin to lose your focus.

What is dangerous is that you confront a player with unrealistic expectations from a pro point of view and, because you are important to the player, he or she might try to answer to them, disturbing his or her balance and blurring his or her goals.

Parting Words: How to Coach Respect

Whether you're coaching a player or you're a player coaching yourself, it's important to teach and learn respect—respect for your opponent, for your surroundings, and for yourself.

Here are five tips to show, and learn, respect:

1. **Accept the moment**. Whatever happens, good or bad, believable or unbelievable, predictable or surprising, accept it, understand it, and then adapt and move on. Disrespect causes us to disbelieve what we're seeing. If we've prejudged (i.e., disrespected) a player as poor or weak or not on our level, we can be quickly surprised when his or her game surpasses our expectations. If we've given another player too much esteem in our minds (i.e., disrespected ourselves), then we can be disbelieving and slow to act when he or she underperforms. Both scenarios adversely affect our level of play.

2. **Focus on what to do now**. Forget the past, forget the future, and simply focus on the now. Respect the moment for what it is, how it's playing out, and

focus on what to do now, not what you didn't do before or should do later.

3. **React to all useful information.** Whatever information you receive, react to it accordingly. What we hear from our "inner circle" isn't always what we see on the court. Old films of a player aren't always accurate as to the player's level of play now, today. Take the information as it comes and assess it for usefulness.

4. **Don't cloud your judgment.** Listening to rumors or feeling overconfident because your inner circle has disrespected an opponent only clouds your judgment. Being open to all information (see above) and assessing it for yourself allows you to remain clear and focused (see below) during play.

5. **Stay focused.** Above all, stay focused on the object at hand, which is simply to win. That is why disrespect is so harmful to inexperienced players: it gets in the way of success.

6. **Don't take anything personal.** Finally, play it off. Things are said, tempers flare, and personalities clash. All you can do is play your best game on that particular day and wash the rest off in the locker room afterward. The more you depend on yourself,

respect yourself, and challenge yourself to your best game play, the less petty comments, politics, and interference from other players, coaches, or umpires will affect you.

This is a very important aspect to consider in the way to respect your emotional stability. Most of the times what people do does affect you, but they are doing it out of what they want, not because it necessarily benefits or damages you. People generally want to win to get into the next round, not to eliminate you from the tournament (though that is the result). It is not personal. We see inexperienced players look angrily at an opponent because he or she just hit an ace. We always wonder why they did that. What, are they angry because they're playing so well?

Most of the time, if someone tries to break your rhythm or tries to steal some points (on low-level tournaments), he or she is doing it out of fear. These opponents are afraid their level might not be good enough to beat you. Handling this strategy is important to win. Most of the time, taking it personally will just make you angry, changing it to a fear-anger contest and giving them exactly what they want.

Chapter 4: *Self-Confidence*

Confidence is a funny thing. Not enough, and you'll never reach your full potential. Too much, and you become overconfident, going for too much, too soon and adjusting too late. And yet, we can't succeed without any confidence at all.

So where is the solution? As with most things, the key to self-confidence lies somewhere in the middle.

The Danger in Positive Thinking

A lot of people think you can build up self-confidence simply by positive thinking. But, in our experience, if you just try to block out the negative or "think good thoughts" or run away from the reality of a current situation, you tend to get a distorted picture of reality.

Reality is a very big part of confidence. When we see players with very little confidence but a lot of potential, we know that we have to get them to believe in their skills before they can fully develop them. Likewise, we see a lot of junior players who have a lot of potential, just not quite as much potential as their overconfidence leads them to believe. We have to spend just as much time with them getting those players to see their true strengths and weaknesses, not just what they've been led to believe.

The difference between your actual skills and your perceived skills can be distorted depending on your level of confidence. Too little confidence, and you think you're worse than you actually are. Too much, and you're not quite as good as you think you are.

Either way, distortions knock you off balance and, as we all know, the more balanced you are, the more in control—and professional—your play will eventually be.

Two Ends of the Confidence Spectrum

Others can add to this distortion as well. If you begin to believe what others say on the positive side, you might wind up a bit blinded as to your own capabilities.

Remember, you can't *play great* if you can't *see straight*. When others pump up your confidence to the extreme, you can begin to think you're as great as people say and possibly overextend yourself, trying things in matches you can't quite achieve based on your current technical skills.

When this happens, you're setting yourself up to fail.

Don't get us wrong—there is nothing wrong with positive thinking. Indeed, positivity is one of the greatest tools available to you as a tennis player. The problem occurs when positive thinking replaces logical thinking and one gets overconfident as a result.

So that's one end of the spectrum: overconfidence. The other end of the spectrum is lack of confidence. People who lack confidence hear the same messages as confident people do— "You can do it," "You're a great player," "You're better than your opponent"—and yet they are full of doubt.

Whenever people tell them they "can" do a thing, their subconscious weighs in and says, "Of course you can't do that. You know you can't do that. You're not good enough."

This lack of confidence leads to doubt, and doubt is a true potential killer. And no tennis player can afford to diminish his or her own potential.

Clearly, there is a difference between what you say and what you believe. You can even try to psych yourself up with positive affirmations and the like, but if you sincerely don't believe them, your mind and your body will never make the connection.

On the other hand, if you believe it falsely—meaning you're more confident than you should be based on your actual abilities—overconfidence can do more harm than good.

If the people you trust build you up too high and, in fact, you yourself build up big positive thoughts about things you are good at but not that good at, your personality, confidence, and skill will start to lean on this, trusting it to be great when it may only be average.

But if these "awesome, best great things" in matches turn out to be "not so good" under tour pressure, your whole sense of confidence will crumble and fall apart, leaving you only with helplessness. It's very important to think positively, but it's also very important that the things you think about are real.

What happens with a lot of good players is that nobody keeps them in perspective, let alone tell them the truth. If they win, everyone around them tells them how great they are. They win some junior tournaments, and everyone thinks they are close to conquering the pro tour. Confidence is good if it is based on skills, skills you still have under pressure.

As a junior, you have to learn to solve your skill limitations fast. If you have a weakness that can be exploited, the pro tour will need only three to six months to find out. So that's the time you will have to solve it. Blinding yourself with false self-confidence will kill you on the pro tour.

Your Inner Circle and Self-Confidence

Who is in your inner circle has a lot to do with your self-confidence. That's because the people in your inner circle have a lot of influence over your state of mind.

If you have negative people in your inner circle, they can create a negative influence and, vice versa, if your inner circle is full of positive people, they will tend to have a positive influence.

It all boils down to you and how you respond to your inner circle. In the last chapter we discussed who to listen to and how often, and even how, to listen to them. This section needs to be a gentle reminder that when people tell you

- "You're much better than this guy."
- "Your serve is the best we've ever seen!"
- "There's no way you can lose!"
- "We're so impressed with your backhand!"
- "You always do great on clay courts!"
- "You have nothing to lose. You are one year younger."
- "You can be top ten in the world."

… they obviously want what's best *for* you, they want to believe it *about* you, and, most of all, they want you to believe it. But only you can determine if it's true or not.

Maybe it just "seems" as if you do well on clay courts because you won your last match, and your inner circle has conveniently forgotten the last four matches you lost on clay.

That's the thing about your inner circle: they tend to deal in generalities. We all know that things aren't "always" the "best." We talked earlier in this book about the power of words, and saying things like "never," "always," "best," and "worst" don't really address the realities of day-to-day tennis play.

The True Meaning of Self-Confidence

The meaning of true, full self-confidence means that you're aware of what you really can—and can't—do. Your focus is on the real skills that you have, not necessarily those that your parents, family, friends, or inner circle say you have.

You have to start with the truth. Maybe you have a lot of potential, but you're not playing up to that. A good coach, an honest coach, a coach who wants to see that potential payoff, won't just list your strengths but will call out your weaknesses too.

It may seem counterproductive to know your weaknesses, but knowing what you can't (yet) accomplish gives you not only the desire to achieve a particular goal but also the knowledge of the right way to handle something.

When you play tennis, you have only so many weapons in your arsenal: a strong backhand, a powerful serve, endurance, stamina, whatever the case may be. Consciously knowing that you have a weak backhand either makes you strengthen it or compensate for it by using your forehand instead. However, thinking you have a strong backhand when you really don't (i.e., overconfidence) means you use it often—and fail often.

On the other hand, knowing you have a weak backhand typically makes the strong player even stronger by working to turn that weakness into a strength.

No one wants an Achilles heel out on the court; you want to be firing on all cylinders, practicing good habits, and using every weapon/tool in your arsenal. To have a pronounced weakness not only makes you a weaker player but your opponent a stronger one by noticing it and playing to it. That's why it's so important to know the reality of your current level of play. You have to know what you can do right now, today, when you step out onto that court. You also have to understand that today's weakness can become tomorrow's strength, but only if you have enough self-confidence—but not too much—to recognize it, work on it, and eliminate it as a weakness.

You also need to focus on how you handle pressure. We all know that there are shots we can make, angles we can take when the pressure is low, that would become more difficult, even impossible, under pressure. Self-confidence gives us the understanding and wisdom to know what we can do under pressure and what we can't.

Striking the Balance between Self-Confidence and Overconfidence: Five Tools to Help

We talked earlier in this chapter about balance—finding it, having it, keeping it. Striking the balance between self-confidence and overconfidence is no different, and here are five tools to help you do just that:

1. **Bring the whole picture into focus.** When it comes to self-confidence, the main thing is to have a really clear picture of your own skills—not as you wish them to be, not as you want them to be, but as they are, right now, in the here and now. Don't just focus on the positive, although that's important; focus on the negative as well. See the whole picture and use it in perspective.

2. **Know your strengths *and* weaknesses.** It's vitally important to know what your strengths and weaknesses are. Knowing what you're strong in helps you emphasize those strengths against your opponents, but it's equally vital that you know your weaknesses as well, to protect and use them as effectively as you can.

3. **Be one step ahead of your weaknesses.** Many players start on the pro tour and make a big impact. Remember, the pro tour generally takes something like three to six months to find out your weaknesses. So you have three to six months to fix them, making yourself less vulnerable. When you know your weaknesses, your coaches and trainers can push on them to make you less weak in those areas. Know them, use them, and prepare to defend them. This way you do stay one step ahead of your opponent.

4. **Never stop learning.** Why is it important to know your strengths and weaknesses? So you can keep developing both. Our ability to learn about ourselves is one of the key indicators of those players who will reach their potential and those who never will. Good players never stop learning. Even those at the top of their game take something away from each match, a nugget or a kernel of understanding to help them improve their game. Your opponents are constantly looking for solutions, so stay in the process, see what you need to improve, and adjust if necessary.

5. **Listen to others with a grain of salt.** If everyone around you is afraid to tell the truth, discourage you, or disappoint you, they will naturally fill your

head with positive images. Most of them think they're trying to help, but they can do more harm than good. Learn to filter out the messages that share opinions and judgments ("great," "super," "awesome," "always," etc.) and focus instead on the facts: your forehand was a little weak, you ran out of steam in the second set, etc.

Confidence is important for every player, because only when you are fully self-confident about your game will you unlock your real potential. Unfortunately, without balance in our lives, we often flit from being overconfident to having no confidence at all.

Self-confidence is the place you find between too much and too little confidence, a surety of your skills and the knowledge of where you are, talent-wise, in the here and now. And knowing where you are is critical for taking the next step toward fulfilling your potential: playing in the Zone!

Chapter 5: The Zone

The Zone puts it all together—every lesson you've learned, every chapter you've read, every skill, habit, strength, or weakness we've talked about in this book.

Sure, sounds great so far, but what exactly *is* the Zone?

The Zone is this perfect state of mind that a tennis player or pro sports player has when he or she is playing at his or her best. That doesn't happen that often, maybe one in every ten matches or so. But the good news is, the closer you stay to the Zone, the better your play is every time you step on the court.

You don't arrive in the Zone by accident; you get there by mastery of play. And, as we've discussed, mastery of play is achieved by controlling your emotions and developing strong lifelong habits on and off the court.

It's Not Perfection—It's the Perfect State of Play

We know it's hard to achieve perfection, but we've all experienced that "perfect" match where everything went our way. Where time seemed to stand still, where the tennis ball seemed as big as a balloon—and just as easy to hit—and where there was a fluid flow from what we sensed to how we reacted to it.

That's the Zone—that "perfect" state of play for our individual talents, strengths, and level of confidence. We call it "perfect" because that's what it feels like inside the Zone, tennis in a perfect state. It doesn't mean you don't make mistakes; you just react to those mistakes, compensate for them, and hopefully overcome them in one long, continuous flow.

The Zone doesn't happen every time we step onto the court. In fact, for most players, it only happens once in every eight or nine matches. But the closer we live to the Zone—the more we work on our game, our emotions, our temper, and our emotional balance—the easier it is to enter the Zone. So even in those nine out of ten matches where we're not fully in the Zone, we still want to play at our best and "live close to" the Zone. So in these nine matches we will have moments, games, or even sets in the Zone and stay close to it in the rest.

There are three main elements to the Zone:

1. **A total absence of time.** This means that you don't think in the past and you don't think in the future; you only think in the now. The more the past enters

the game, it takes you out of the Zone. The more you're worried about, or pressured by, the future, the sooner you leave the Zone.

2. **A total absence of judgment.** You're not thinking in terms of "good" and "bad" in the Zone. The minute you stop to think, "Hey, that was a good shot" or "Man, I'm playing so badly today," you're probably already out of the Zone and back into conscious thinking again. It's about playing, period. Playing, not judging. No good, not great, just play to win. Play in the moment.

3. **A total unity of the senses.** When you're in the Zone, your senses are heightened and working together. You're seeing things, hearing things, feeling things, and reacting to them. You might experience the following: you see the ball very clear and big, you hear its sound "full" when you strike the ball, you are always in time for every shot, you feel everything about the contact with the ball. This happens repeatedly throughout the match. It's a constant flow of seeing, hearing, feeling, sensing, and reacting to things. Again, it's not a conscious effort but an unconscious "flow" of sensing and reacting, sensing and reacting.

To more fully see what it's like playing in the Zone, let's study each of these three levels more closely:

A Total Absence of Time

The Zone is living in the moment. All your focus is available on the present moment so that you can react using all your senses.

When you say things like, "Oh, this is my third double fault of the match," you're already making an overview of the past. If you're thinking, "Ah, one more shot and I have a match point," then you're thinking ahead in the future that it's nearly impossible to be "present" in the present.

These things tend to snowball. If you're up 5–1 and then you're 5–5 and now you're thinking, "Oh, this is the third match this year where I can't close the deal and take him out." You can go way back even further, and the further you're back in the past, the weaker your play in the present will be.

You can also fast-forward to the future and have thoughts like, "Am I good enough to make it?" Of course, there are moments to reflect on the past and assess your chances for the future. But many inexperienced players and members of their inner circle take the opportunity to talk about the future after *every* lost match, especially after big losses: "If you play like this, you can never be in the top 200."

Every top player has some very bad matches every year. Most of the time, taking these moments to assess the chances for the future is very counterproductive. Playing a match around these kinds of contemplations will for sure not make it easy to focus on the now.

Any thought that involves time will distract you from focusing totally on the moment. When you're totally focused *on* the moment, interesting things happen *in* the moment. That's because the fewer distractions you have in the moment, the longer that moment feels.

It's incredibly freeing to play in the Zone and focus totally in the present—to not drag all those past mistakes and future pressures into the match, to just play each point for point and focus on the solutions to whatever problems may arise.

Time seems to slow down inside the Zone. From being pressured and rushed outside the Zone, you suddenly have all the time in the world to focus on the strokes you need to take to return the ball or serve the ball, whatever the case may be.

We've heard players say that inside the Zone, the ball even seems bigger. One player described it as being "as big as a melon" and that visualization allowed her to focus solely on returning it effectively, i.e., it seemed much easier to hit.

From the outside looking in, it can appear as if you're moving very fast and your handling speed is incredible, but there, inside the Zone, it feels like just the opposite, as if you almost have all the time in the world to accomplish your goals and win the match.

A Total Absence of Judgment

You can't judge while in the Zone. To judge is to step back from the moment, to step outside the Zone and label something as "good," "bad," "excellent," or "horrible."

These three elements of being in the Zone all work together. You can't have a total absence of time without a total absence of judgment, because to judge literally means to stop the progress and momentum of what you're doing and assess the situation in a negative or positive manner.

Judgments are measurements, and to measure you must stop and think what just happened, but to "stop" at all is to step out of the Zone. And that's the opposite of what we want you to do.

A Total Unity of the Senses

There is a delicate connection inside the Zone that comes when all the senses are working together and funneling straight into action. Just like the total absence of time or judgment, there must be an uninterrupted flow of activity.

Outside the Zone, there is a lot of processing going on. You see something, and then you stop to assess it. You hear something, and then you pause before reacting. Inside the Zone, it all happens fluidly. There is no time, or need, to consciously pause before reacting.

You see, you react.

You hear, you react.

You sense something, you react to it.

Again, this fluid connection is directly linked to and influenced by the previous two elements of playing in the Zone.

This instant reaction gives you access to understanding your own technical level of play as well as your opponent's. This allows you to more easily predict what your opponent will do and how your opponent will act, in order for you to move and play accordingly.

Living the Zone

Your goal as a tennis player, from beginner to pro, is to be in the Zone—or as close to the Zone—*as often as possible.*

Everything we've taught you up to now has been with the express purpose of bringing you close to the Zone. Experience, the acceptance-action response, respect—all these skills are tools you can use to bring yourself closer to the Zone with each match. That's why we try to teach our players positive habits where they don't disrespect themselves or others, judge themselves or others, or rely too closely on their inner circle to not unrealistically change their balance of confidence.

When you play habitually in an honest frame of mind, you move closer to the Zone. When you rely on emotions, get angry, call yourself "stupid," or lose control, you move further and further away from the Zone.

The further away from the Zone you are, the less often you play there. So if a healthy, well-adjusted, habitual player is in the Zone three or four times out of every ten matches, a player who lives far away from the Zone only gets to play there every fifteen or twenty matches.

Conclusion: Don't Just Play in the Zone, Live There

The habits we've discussed in this book aren't designed to just create winners on the court but winners in life as well. These are all good habits that will improve every area of the life you want to lead. On the job, in school, at home, and in relationships, the more balance, control, and skills you have, the richer, happier, and more satisfying your life will be.

Life is full of pressure. Be it on the job or in school, in your relationships, or in your extracurricular activities, being able to handle your emotions helps you excel in all matters of your life.

Remember that the Zone exists off the court as well. You can be in the Zone anywhere and everywhere, in every aspect of your life:

- In a relationship, you can experience times when everything is going right.

- On the job, you can give a presentation or deliver a project where things just go your way.

- Maybe you are in a presentation reacting to the people in the room. Even before they can articulate their questions, you react in a flowing way and naturally involve them without thinking.

- In school, you can have a perfect day—or class period—where time seems to slow down, every answer is easy, every grade is good, and understanding comes easily as well.

- In the office you might be working on an interesting piece and words just flow onto your paper; you have the whole concept in your head just rushing to get it on paper, forgetting time. When you are finished, and you realize it is a few hours later, you think, "Wow, how is this possible? It seems like I just started on it!"

These are all examples of how we go in and out of the Zone in our lives as well as in our favorite sport.

One Hand Washes the Other

Have you ever heard the expression "One hand washes the other"? This means that you can't wash your left hand without washing your right, and vice versa. Likewise, you can't benefit from playing in the Zone if you don't try to live there off the court as well.

The Zone is not some magical place you hop in and out of when you feel like it; it's a habit more than anything, a way of playing in the moment that comes from practice—lots and lots of practice. And that practice comes on and off the court.

If you don't live in the Zone—if you're chaotic, emotional, dramatic, depressed, and excitable in your daily life—it's not very realistic to think that you'll suddenly flip a switch and be completely different when you step onto the tennis court. That doesn't make sense.

Daily life isn't that different from tennis; you have your good days and your bad, your strengths and weaknesses, your ups and downs. But, just like in tennis, there is a lot of life that you can predict. Take traffic, for instance. Anyone with a driver's license knows that traffic exists—it's no big surprise. We also know that people tend to lose their manners, their grace, and their logic when they get behind the wheel. So it should come as no surprise on your daily commute to and from work that not only will there be traffic, but people will be ugly; they'll cut you off, they'll steal your parking space, they'll tailgate you, they won't use their blinkers, and they'll speed and stop up, seemingly for no reason.

To get frustrated and angry, to get emotional, and to have "road rage" is to take yourself far away from the Zone, particularly when you know and can predict that this is going to happen. Why? Because it happens (almost) every day.

Getting agitated and angry simply doesn't solve the problem. Living in the Zone means that you assess every situation in the moment—not just in a game, set, or match but in life as well. If the driver in front of you is slamming on his or her brakes every ten seconds, why stay behind that driver? Why put yourself through that irritation if you can avoid it? Switch lanes and pass him or her and wait to assess the next obstacle or impediment to your progress.

Living in the Present Tense

There is a time for planning, for preparation, and for goal setting. As coaches, we spend a lot of time here because this is all skill building, but even we know that you can't just build your skills forever. Eventually, you have to rely on the skills you've built, the goals you've set and met, and the planning and preparation you've done and use them in the present tense.

There is also a time for looking at the past to revisit what happened, to see how we responded to it and to learn from that. We can also plan for the future by working out and assessing our future. In tennis we study our opponents and where our next match will be, finding out what needs to be planned. But if you're spending too much time in the past or are too focused on the future, then living in the present tense is going to be more challenging for you when it's time to actually get down to business.

Where you spend your time is a habit, like everything else. If you worry too much about the past, that's where you're spending much of your time, and that becomes habitual. If you're too focused on the future, always dreaming or goal setting or planning, you become preoccupied with the future at the cost of the present.

Life, and living inside the Zone, is about balance—a healthy balance between respect for the past, knowledge about the future, but mostly how often you live in the present tense. If your life is out of balance, you'll be too far in the past or too far in the future and not "present" enough in the present tense.

(Don't) You Be the Judge

Being judgmental is another one of those "bad habits" that takes you right out of the Zone. We live in a judgmental society. So much of life is based on appearance, weight, fitness, fashion, and who is "cool" or "uncool."

With our junior players, in particular, they are almost programmed to make snide comments or judgments about people, on and off the court. This too is a habit that we have in daily life and that spills over onto the court.

So what can you do if you're too judgmental about others? You can start by recognizing the problem. Notice how you act toward others, when they're in or out of your presence. If you and your friends start talking about a person the minute they leave the room, wow, yes, you're probably too judgmental.

If you walk down the street with a friend and most of your conversation is spent ragging on others about their appearance or fashion sense or how much money they may or may not have, then that is something to watch out for, be careful of, and work hard to rectify.

Judgment is really about negativity. It's about putting someone else down to make yourself feel better. What is trash talk but a way to make yourself feel stronger by trying to make your opponent feel weaker? But we can tell you from experience that trash talk only makes you the weaker opponent because it generally reflects the opinion that you have to resort to trash talk because your play isn't strong enough to overcome your opponent on its own. Pro players know this, and so they usually avoid trash talk at all costs.

Another important point about judging is there are a lot of people who judge all the time, all day. We tried this with students and their parents, asking them how many times they judge during a day. Often the outcome was "all the time, all day long."

So here is the point: if you are judging everything and everyone all day, together with your friends, who also do it, then everyone sees this as normal behavior. So if you do something that other people see, you think it is natural that everyone is judging you. This does make you very aware of yourself in the eyes of others. When you're operating in this kind of an emotional climate, it's nearly impossible to not judge yourself, get insecure, or focus on the present without thinking, "What will everybody say and think of it?"

When this happens, you are *way* out of the Zone.

Negativity also keeps you out of the Zone. It's okay to think certain things—we can't help how we react or immediately feel about someone—but we can influence our emotions by analyzing why we have such a strong reaction to an opponent or a stranger on the street. If we can learn to observe and let go without judgment, to just be our own person and not worry about how much money other people have, how much they weigh, or where they bought their clothes, then we keep the focus on us and not on the negativity we feel for others.

One thing we try to teach our students (and ourselves) is the life lesson that "you can be for somebody without being against somebody." Trash-talking and hoping that an opponent double-faults takes a lot of the focus off of you and your game; it also takes a lot of energy, leaving us unprepared for the next shot. Don't spend your energy rooting against others, because living in the Zone requires all the energy and attention you've got.

Pro players know that life is a journey, not a destination. This takes some of the time pressure and judgment out of their game. They know that if they do lose a game, it's not just because their opponent is a "bad guy" but because, on that day, the opponent was simply better prepared, or played better, than they did. Good players know that the only life they can control—the only game they can control—is their own, and that's where they put their energy, their focus, and their balance.

Parting Words about Living in the Zone

Most of us who love tennis make it a significant part of our lives. You could almost say that we "live and breathe" tennis. As a junior and as you move forward in your tennis career, don't shy away from this trend. Know that what makes you a better player on the court is directly linked to what makes you a better person off the court—and vice versa.

Remember that the habits you have in your daily life, where you spend your energy and time—in the past, present, or future— all come back to how you play the game. We encourage you to live in the Zone because that makes it easier for you to play in the Zone.